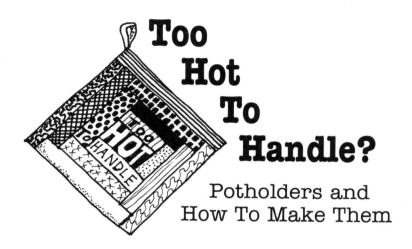

Too Hot To Handle?

Potholders and How To Make Them

OTHER BOOKS AVAILABLE FROM CHILTON
Robbie Fanning, Series Editor

Too Hot To Handle?

Potholders and How To Make Them

Doris Lyons Hoover

Chilton Book Company
Radnor, Pennsylvania

KALEIDO
CRAFT
·SCOPE·

Manufactured in the United States of America

Library of Congress Cataloging in Publication Data
Hoover, Doris.
    Too hot to handle? : potholders and how to make them / Doris Lyons
  Hoover.
       p.   cm.
    Includes index.
    ISBN 0-8019-8381-9
    1. Potholders. 2. Potholders—History. 3. Textile crafts.
  I. Title.
  TT699.H64   1993
  746.9—dc20   93-21696
                                           CIP

1 2 3 4 5 6 7 8 9 0   2 1 0 9 8 7 6 5 4 3

Contents

CONTENTS

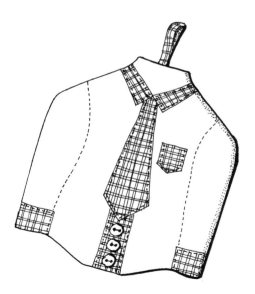

Foreword

Go ahead and unleash your snickers. Doris Hoover and I are used to it. We know what you're saying because we've heard it before: *A whole book on potholders? You must be joking!*

I think she and I should start a society to combat size-ism. I'd call it HOLDER— Help Original Little Designs Earn Respect.

Do you laugh at a whole book on jewelry?
Jewelry is small and unique—*just like potholders.*

Do you dismiss collections of thimbles?
They're all the same, yet different— *just like potholders.*

Do you make fun of bonsai?
They'll outlive you—*just like potholders.*

Merely because it's small and lives in the kitchen doesn't mean it doesn't deserve respect. Hail to the lowly potholder!

It's the perfect size for 30-minute projects, brings a thumbprint of creativity to your kitchen, makes an ideal hostess or wedding gift, can be interpreted as artistically as quilts and other softworks, is a place to recycle materials and test battings, has a fascinating history, and can masquerade as an eyeglass holder and other items.

Best of all, its champion is Doris Hoover, a woman who brings whimsy, creativity, and beauty to everything she does.

So go ahead and laugh. But you'll be missing a wonderful little book. Meanwhile, Doris and I will hold a society meeting and finish a potholder while you're giggling.

Robbie Fanning
Series Editor

Are you interested in a quarterly newsletter about creative uses of the sewing machine, serger, and knitting machine? Write to The Creative Machine-s, PO Box 2634, Menlo Park, CA 94026.

Acknowledgments

My sincere thanks to:

Friends, artists, and collectors, who have lent their potholders and their support, especially Winder Baker, Patricia Boucher, Marcia Breon, Diane Conradson, Dagmar Dern, Ann DeWitt, Mairy DeWitt, Phyllis Dukes, Marilyn Green, Eli Leon, Clydine Peterson, Dorothea Pursell, Bets Ramsey, Brant Ward, Ray Ward, Janie Warnick, and William Woys Weaver.

Tamis Hoover Renteria, for convincing me that I could use a word processor and for patient help early in this project.

Inez Brooks-Meyers, Associate Curator of Costume and Textiles, Oakland Museum, Oakland, California, for information, advice, and encouragement.

Teachers and students of past years, from whom I have learned much of what I know.

Robbie Fanning, who gave me the courage to try.

Shawn and Tegan Hoover, for help in collecting potholders and information and for untying a few of my computer knots.

My husband, for support and good humor.

Potholders are quiet items and people are quiet about them. When was the last time you had a conversation about potholders? Yet I know there are many potholder stories, collections, and makers out there that you know about. I'd like to hear about them. Write to me at P.O. Box 2634, Menlo Park, California, 94026.

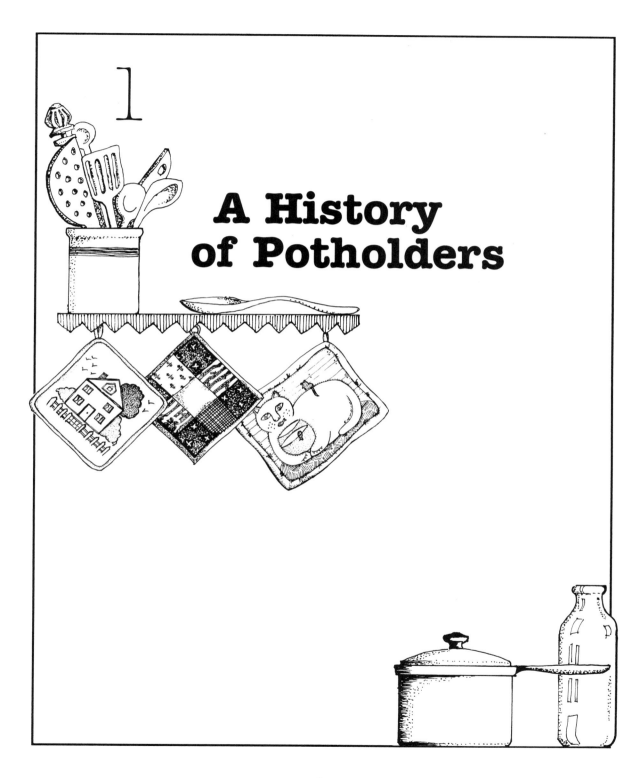

1

A History of Potholders

Potholders from the Past

The history of potholders is hidden in the smoke of many past cooking fires. No one thought them important enough to document before the 1900s. No housewife mentioned them in her household inventory nor did any cook will a potholder to her heirs. Few remain from previous generations; they were used until they wore thin or were scorched and burned beyond use and then were simply thrown away. These neglected items fall with many others into the category of anonymous women's arts.

Although antique potholders are rare, a few have found their way to museums, such as the National Museum of American History at the Smithsonian Institution in Washington, D.C. Two from the eighteenth century are linen embellished with crewel embroidery; the one dated 1774 is the oldest potholder I have located (Fig. 1-1). Another from the late nineteenth century is silk with silk embroidery. While such elegant materials rarely saw hard use, one of the linen ones is indeed a well-worn potholder. They were apparently from genteel homes, perhaps made as gifts for a new bride.

Fig. 1-1.
Left, a potholder from Pennsylvania dated 1774. Right, potholder from the Copp family in Stonington, Connecticut, also circa the late eighteenth century. Both are crewel embroidery on linen. Collection Smithsonian Institution.

In *American Quilts: A Handmade Legacy*, the catalogue to an impressive show at the Oakland Museum in Oakland, California, Rachel Maines states that "Personal objects . . . such as hand-knitted sanitary napkins and potholders, have generally been considered unsuitable for acquisition by museums." However, a footnote by the editor tells us that "in 1990 . . . a founding curator of the Oakland Public Museum collected an early 19th Century patchwork potholder to complete a period 'kitchen' exhibit" (Fig. 1-2).

In this same catalogue, a picture from the archives of the Minnesota Historical Society shows World War I Junior Red Cross girls displaying potholders they made. How this helped the war effort is questionable, but it taught the girls basic sewing skills. Perhaps stitching the potholders prepared them for assembling the stacked patchwork quilts shown in the same scene, as similar techniques are employed in making both items.

Housed in the collections at the Winterthur Museum in Delaware is a blue-and-white potholder, most probably worked as a learning project (Fig. 1-3). Silk cross-stitches on white cotton carefully proclaim, "Nancy Mason is my name. New England is my station. Cumberland is my dwelling place and Christ is my salvation." Nancy dates her work "March 30 AD 1814." The reverse side is a carefully stitched star also worked in a cross-stitch. One can envision a young girl stitching tediously, biting her lip while stifling tears and occasionally sucking a needle-pricked finger—all in her struggle to attain the perfection expected of her.

Another "kettle holder" worked to perfect embroidery technique was given

Fig. 1-2.
A red print is pieced with a wavy stripe of brown and cream in this cotton hot pad. The back is a seersuckerlike stripe of blue and ecru. The binding is straight grain. Probably circa the late nineteenth century. Collection Oakland Museum.

Fig. 1-3.
A sampler potholder made in 1814, the blue silk embroidery is on a white cotton ground. Courtesy, Winterthur Museum.

in 1867 to a friend of her family by seven-year-old Jenny Morris, daughter of William Morris, the designer and advocate of fine handcrafts, such as meticulous needlework.

Potholders in surprising numbers have survived from the turn of the century, surfacing at flea markets, estate sales, and antiques shops, more often in the eastern part of the United States— in New England and in the Pennsylvania-German area of Pennsylvania. In the collection of Marcia Breon, gathered principally in the East, patchwork dominates, testifying to its age by the use of fabrics typical of that era. Some are cotton while others are wool, with one surprise piece worked in the softly aged colors of needlepoint yarns. Marcia has two unusual pieces from this same period (Fig. 1-4). The images are of fowl, both in an upright posture and seemingly made to perch on a teapot's hot handle. The chicken, from Pennsylva-

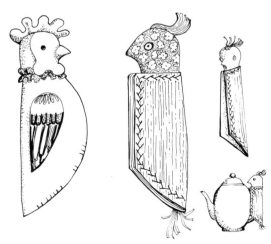

Fig. 1-4.
Birds at attention help pour tea. Collection Marcia Breon.

nia, is of felt in the soft colors of gray, violet, rust, rose, and yellow-orange, with wool and cotton embroidery and eyes of yellow-green beads. The other bird is much more flamboyant, fashioned of elegant taffeta and printed corduroys with a brilliant pearl cotton—tufted comb and tail and rhinestone eyes.

Patricia T. Herr, in an article about small items made with quilting techniques in Pennsylvania-German households, describes an unusually frivolous Amish hot-pot holder—circa the twentieth century—of red wool trimmed with velvet ribbon and bound with grosgrain silk ribbon. Its round layers are tied together by colorful wool yarns which are decorative as well as functional.

During the late 1930s and early 1940s, when most women were primarily homemakers and attitudes were still influenced by memories of the Great Depression, women's magazines featured numerous how-to articles geared to making inexpensive gifts for others or to making one's own surroundings more gracious with little expenditure. Potholders were often featured as simple projects, taking the form of perky chickens, Cape Cod cottages in gingham, or pieces of fruit often tucked into a basket-shaped container. Mirroring the casually insulting racial clichés of that era, three Black Mammy potholders housed in a watermelon-shaped holder are a documentation of their time and thus have become desirable today to collectors of African-American memorabilia.

Patricia Hubbell Boucher owns a unique group of hot pads rescued from an attic in Syracuse, New York, all apparently made by one person, perhaps in the 1920s but surely by the 1930s. Similar in style and mostly in pairs, they appear to have been kits printed for embroidery. Each hangs from a cream-colored plastic ring. Among them are "A Book for the Cook" and a Dutch boy and girl (Fig. 1-5). Another piece from Pat's collection is unfinished, with the needle and embroidery thread still attached, and bears the name of the company that printed its teacup design along its edge: Potholder No. 358A—JBK Co.

When were potholders first commercially produced? In an 1895 *Montgomery Ward Catalogue*, potholders are not mentioned, but by 1902, Sears Roebuck offers an asbestos flatiron holder for handling flatirons and hot dishes at a price of five cents each. In *Shaker Textile Arts*, Beverly Gordon tells us that in a Shaker community catalogue, probably from

Fig. 1-5.
These potholders were probably made from commercial kits. Collection Patricia Hubbell Boucher.

the 1920s, potholders were listed by that name.

Most older persons, when questioned, have little recollection of what they or their mothers used to protect their hands from the searing heat of pan and pot handles in earlier years, though Violet Pannell, who grew up in rural Alabama in the early part of this century, remembers using cotton flour sacks, usually folded over several times. Eula Boggs, also from northern Alabama, made 7"-square potholders from worn overall legs. My copy of a 1946 edition of *Cooking Out-of-Doors*, published by the Girl Scouts, suggests including in your camping equipment a large kerchief or bandanna to use as a pot lifter.

William Woys Weaver, a food researcher from Pennsylvania, has remembrances of his own and stories from kinswomen about potholders. According to Mr. Weaver's grandmother, her great-aunt, Lydia, who insisted on cooking at an open hearth as late as 1915, used only rags as potholders because the cloth was constantly getting scorched and blackened, a fact probably true for many women in primitive kitchens. From his own childhood in Pennsylvania, Mr. Weaver remembers a woman who sold potholders door-to-door, with some of her creations woven from grass or reeds, which were pliant as cloth.

Paradise Lost, Potholders Found

From layers of grasses, rags, flour sacks, kerchiefs, worn overalls, and thick towels to the folded hem of a generously proportioned apron or perhaps a simple padded square, all of these naive and unheralded improvisations were forerunners of today's decorator potholders.

As an example of the obscurity to which potholders have been relegated, in a search of the five English-French dictionaries available in my local library, I found no mention of potholders. Obviously, the editors were not cooks or they would have included this vital piece of kitchen equipment.

Since there seems to be no written history of the origin of potholders, we might imagine our own whimsical version:

Adam was probably around a few millennia before Eve came along to liven up his life, which until then had been pretty dull. When Eve came on the scene, she introduced Adam to many new and exciting experiences, one of them, undoubtedly, being her discovery of fire and its many benefits.

"It warms your toes on an icy morning."

"It dries your bearskin after a downpour."

"It keeps the wolves away."

Eventually, Eve realized that certain morsels of food were improved by contact with the heat of the campfire, and so "cook" was added to her already extensive roles.

"Sweep the cave, wife."

"Burp the baby, wife."

"Gather the acorns, wife."

Since fire was Eve's discovery, it quickly became her responsibility as well.

"Gather wood and build the fire, wife."

"Cook my meat, wife."

It may have been some time before Eve discovered clay pots for cooking, but when she did, she recognized a need to protect her hands from the hot pots and simultaneously invented the potholder.

What was the first one like? It might have been several layers of leaves bunched together or a small animal skin (Fig. 1-6). Whatever it was, present-day potholders are not very different. They are flexible, insulated, compact, utilitarian items. Almost every kitchen contains several: some battered and burned, hidden in a drawer and perhaps a few reserved for show, bright designer pieces hung above the stove for all to see, sophisticated versions of Eve's creation (Fig. 1-7).

Fig. 1-6.
The first potholders?

Fig. 1-7.
These potholders are hung for viewing and easy access.

Potholders Today

Some years ago, I conducted a pot-holder-making class, a lighthearted but productive one-day workshop. In the class description, I suggested that we give potholders some prestige, lift them from the bottom of the kitchen drawer to the top of the counter, and take them beyond mere utility to "almost art."

This challenge, issued today, would seem unnecessary. Though once mundane items, potholders have in recent years reached new levels of glamour. One finds them in gourmet kitchen shops, upscale gift catalogues, and ritzy department stores. They may take the form of a mitten disguised as a fish, eager to grasp a hot handle in his insulated mouth, or a graphic black-and-white-checkered square appealing to those with minimalist taste (Fig. 1-8). One recent holiday season, I ventured into the housewares department of a local store and discovered a rack of potholders. Picking up a bright red one, I noticed a tiny printed directive, "Push me." I did and was amazed to hear "Jingle Bells" electronically rendered. The limitations of the basic square have exploded into the age of technology.

Inspired by the few records we have, cooks and artists with fertile imaginations will find that potholders offer a vast, unthreatening field for their inventive needle skills. As useful and decorative items for the maker's kitchen or as usable gifts that the recipient can quickly scorch to nonrecognition if she doesn't like them, potholders will always be in demand—unless, of course, scientists prove them obsolete by inventing a way to cook without heat. I hope that doesn't happen.

Fig. 1-8.
Hot pads take many forms, from naturalistic fish to stark black-and-white checks.

2 Putting Potholders to Use, Then and Now

The potholder's very name and definition would seem to limit its use to handling hot pots and dishes, but from the times of our grandmothers and great-grandmothers until today, it has served in other roles both utilitarian and frivolous. Perhaps a clue to this wider use is given by the single word "holders" embroidered on decorative pieces made to house "holders" or, as we know them, potholders. (See color section.) "Holders" is non-specific in what is to be held, implying not just pots, but flatirons, stove-eye lifters, or other hot implements. (In the decorative piece referred to above, the potholders are held in place by snaps. More frequently they are tucked into the pocket of a basket-shaped container as seen in Fig. 3-16 in Chapter 3.)

Flatiron Holders, Polishing Cloths, Table Mats

For women of our grandmothers' generation, Monday was wash day and Tuesday was ironing day. There were no drip-dries, no permanent press, no polyester in their day. Everything was natural fiber and had to be ironed. After drying outside on a clothesline, everything was sprinkled with water and rolled up tight for even dampness. Pleats, tucks, ruffles, work shirts, housedresses, your Sunday best—all were then treated to the hot pressure of a flatiron heated on the wood-burning stove or in the embers of the hearth fire (Fig. 2-1). Unfortunately, as the heavy, solid iron absorbed heat, so did its iron

Fig. 2-1.
A potholder gripped the handle of a flatiron like this one to protect one's hands from the heat.

handle. Without protection, the handgrip was too hot to handle, so the potholder came to the rescue, working nonstop on ironing day as the weary housewife alternated irons, switching from a cooling one to a glowing hot one. If you're wondering how they knew when the iron was hot enough, Jacqueline Enthoven tells me that while American women spit on the plate of the iron, judging its temperature by the sizzle, French housewives held the searing plate near their cheek, sensing its degree of heat.

Fortunately, not all potholders are associated with such old-time drudgery, but their compact, flexible form of natural fiber aids in tasks we still perform today. Old, worn potholders are ideal as polishing cloths for furniture or brass. A mitt potholder would make the messy task even easier (Fig. 2-2).

Protecting our hands from hot pans and casseroles has always been the potholder's primary function. Our forebears' heavy iron pots and skillets, heated over an open fire or on a wood stove, demanded potholders for safe handling. Even though many cooking vessels today have composition handles that do not conduct heat and therefore preclude the use of potholders, roasting pans and baking dishes steaming from the oven and overly warm microwave containers do, indeed, dictate the protection given by the humble potholder.

Escaping from the kitchen stove, colorful, well-designed potholders are ideal as hot mats on the dining table, protecting the table surface from heat and moisture, thus serving decoratively as well as functionally (Fig. 2-3).

Fig. 2-2.
A hot mitt adapts easily as a polishing glove.

Batting Samplers, Token Gifts, Christmas Ornaments

To test the effects of different quilt batts, teacher/artist Vicki Johnson begs batting leftovers from her students—just enough to make a potholder—and incorporates them into sample quilted squares, which she labels carefully, denoting the brand and type of batting on the back. The benefits are double: Vicki determines the effect of a specific batting worked in her technique while gaining colorful hot mats ready for emergency service.

As a lighthearted yet practical token gift, a potholder can commemorate a holiday, celebrate a newly decorated kitchen, add a handmade touch to a store-bought gift, or merely evidence your goodwill. Fun to design, easy to make, and fairly quick to complete, they lay no burden on the giver or the recipient: They do not demand display

Fig. 2-3.
Oversize potholders double as hot mats at the table.

on the living room mantle; they are expected to be used; and the giver cannot be distressed if they die in the line of duty. They are also inexpensive to make and are ecologically sound when made from recycled or waste remnants.

A little imagination can produce a unique gift for a particular occasion. Patchwork potholders in Valentine colors and potato-printed fabrics carried greetings to special friends of mine during one February (Fig. 2-4). Recently, after receiving a colorful and original southwestern-style wedding invitation, I tucked a potholder in with the mixing bowls I sent as my gift. Taking my clue from the color and design of the invitation, I assume the potholder I made reflected the taste of the bride and groom. (See color section.)

Genuine love and affection may be conveyed by a handsome gift potholder. A delightful example, made by Carolyn Miller for her children's grandmother, is a refrigerator-hung potholder imprinted with "There's no place like home except G-Mama's," evidence of the important role played by grandmother Lou Miller in the lives of her children and grandchildren.

Of course, sometimes gift potholders are so attractive that one chooses to preserve them, hanging them in a place of honor for all to see and enjoy. Such is the case with a handpainted set of potholders made for my daughter, Tamis, by the children at a day-care center where she worked, guided by Chyerl Hoshida. Ten years

Fig. 2-5.
Bets Ramsey calls this potholder "London Road" and decorated it with buttons found on London pavements.

Fig. 2-4.
February greetings were sent via a patchwork Valentine hot pad.

later, the bright gift potholders still hang in her kitchen, cheerful reminders of her creative child-care friends. (See color section.)

Following a discussion about finding stray buttons anywhere in the world, Bets Ramsey made a potholder decorated with buttons found on the pavements of London (Fig. 2-5). That piece hangs in my living room. She also makes miniature potholders as Christmas tree ornaments for friends (Fig. 2-6). Measuring about 3″ square and worked in reds and greens of scraps previously too small to save, these tiny gems are stitched by hand. Bets packages the precut pieces in plastic sandwich bags and stitches meticulously wherever she may be, from dull meetings to airport lounges.

Fig. 2-6.
These miniature hot pads serve as Christmas tree ornaments. Bets Ramsey.

Advertising, Souvenirs, Invitations

Businesses use potholders as another kind of gift. Printed with advertising slogans or political messages aimed at the homemaker, potholders may urge the purchase of real estate, oil-heating systems, or dry-cleaning services. Even aspiring assemblymen, representatives, and senators have solicited votes through the humble potholder.

The latter practice caused a small controversy in our local California newspaper. A would-be congresswomen solicited the feminine vote through potholders mailed to women only. Letters to the editor appeared nightly as some took offense at this sexist attitude: "Does she think I stay home all day doing nothing but cook[ing]?" However, one women wrote, "I love my potholder. Not only is it a terrific conversation piece but my older son uses it to take hot motorcycle parts out of the oven. If [she] wants to send me an apron, I'd be delighted. I will give it to my younger son, the chef."

In recent years, a new niche has been carved for potholders—that of travel souvenir. Often emblazoned with the name or symbol of their country of origin, they are affordable and easy to slip into a crowded suitcase. Unfortunately, the quality of design or materials is often ignored, in some sense demeaning their home country. Among the more interesting ones are those from Panama, made from fragments of

Kuna molas—bright reverse appliqués—for the tourist trade, and a cotton crochet hot pad in cream, black, and red made by Elsie James, a Hopi woman I met while she was making Indian fry bread at the Heard Museum in Phoenix, Arizona (Fig. 2-7).

Occasionally, you might happen on a treasure for your souvenir. In a small town market in Portugal, I was fortunate to find a woman selling produce from her garden; seemingly as an afterthought, she also displayed potholders made by her own hand. They were truly primitives, naive in selection of color and design. I was delighted and purchased four crochet potholders and two mirror-image embroidered cats (Fig. 2-8). The crochet hot pads were the maker's version of granny squares in amazing color combinations. The cats gazed out from beige wool faces with

Fig. 2-8.
This pair of wool potholders was found in Portugal. Author's collection.

button eyes. They were lined with a blue-gray check wool, the edge finished with a yellow ocher buttonhole stitch. They elicit visions of the Portugal that I wish to remember.

A truly unusual and unexpected use for a souvenir potholder recently occurred in my stitchery group. In a Christmas potholder exchange among the members, Nancy Welch drew the name of Gillian Arnold, a short-term member who will eventually return to her home in England. Nancy's inventive solution for a personal potholder was a photographic image of Gill's American house done in color Xerox transfer and then appliquéd to a background of the Stars and Stripes, a genuine made-in-America souvenir (Fig. 2-9). A few months later, Gill invited the group to her house for lunch. I, as well as several others, found her cul-de-sac but had failed to memorize her house number. Remembering the potholder image,

Fig. 2-7.
Traditional Hopi designs enhance a crocheted potholder. Author's collection.

Fig. 2-9.
A potholder made by Nancy Welch shows the house of recipient Gillian Arnold.

Fig. 2-10.
An unusual party invitation—a potholder.

we peered carefully at the various houses and knew immediately which one to go to.

Here's another unusual potholder use. Who would have thought of a potholder as a party invitation? In her "From Thornhill Farm" magazine column in *House Beautiful*, Dee Hardie tells of sending house-shaped potholders as the invitations to a name-our-new-house party. She pinned the paper invitation to the potholder, but imaginative fiber artists should be able to print the invitation on the potholder, perhaps on the back. Either way, this is an invitation that could not be ignored (Fig. 2-10).

How's this for a clever, offbeat use of a potholder? Along with other symbolic items, such as aspirin for unforeseen headaches and adhesive bandages for damaged feelings, a potholder for hot tempers was included in a survival kit for potential classroom teachers.

Doubtless, homemakers and other creative people have found many innovative uses for potholders other than those described here or in the dictionary. In chapter 6, we will push the boundaries even further by exploring other possibilities.

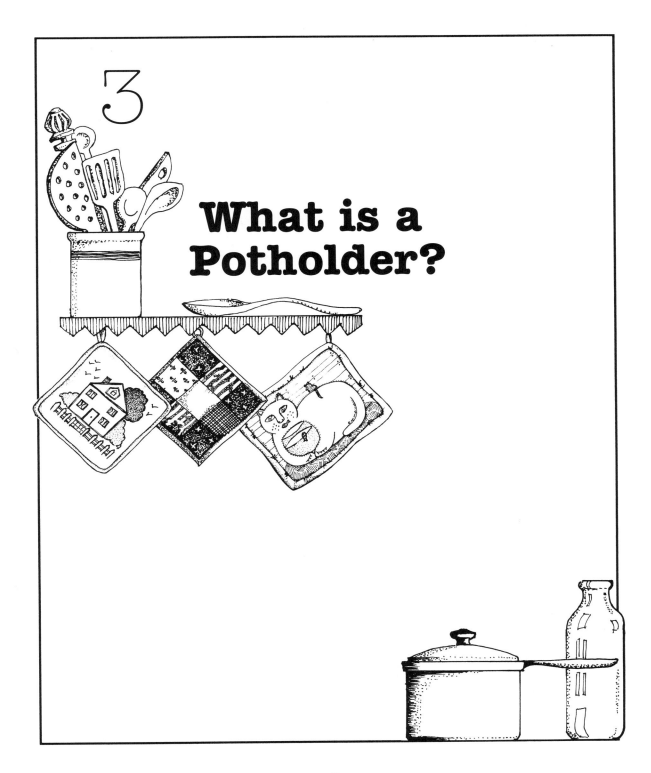

3

What is a Potholder?

What do you envision when you hear the word "potholder?" Some people think of flat ones; others see mitts with or without thumbs; still others envision double mitts. These basic forms can be disguised as strawberries, chickens, melons, and countless other unlikely images and can be fashioned of patchwork, appliqué, quilting, knitting, crochet, and weaving.

Padded Fabric

As we have seen, some of the oldest existing potholders are padded fabric, either patchwork or embroidered. This

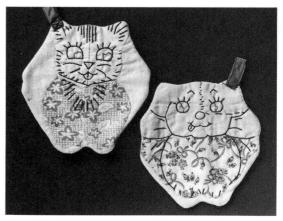

Fig. 3-1.
This gingham dog and calico cat are probably from the 1930s. Author's collection.

Fig. 3-2.
These green-and-white terry cloth hot pads are commercially made. Author's collection.

flat form is still the most popular kind of potholder, given variety by shape and embellishment. An example, probably from the 1930s, is a pair depicting a gingham dog and a calico cat (Fig. 3-1). Cut in free-form shapes, the two animals are carefully appliquéd and embroidered. The fabric is flour sacking and the filler is thin, perhaps a layer of a worn blanket. Another pair of an indeterminate date, though not hand-made, is of thick terry cloth bound with bias tape (Fig. 3-2). The green teapot, cup, and saucer woven into the white background reverse their colors on the back side. They bear a label proclaiming "Ritz Quality," and a rusted metal eyelet allows them to hang from a cup hook.

Though not done so much nowadays, hot-pot holders have often been made in pairs. Occasionally, the mates of a pair of flat potholders are connected by a cord or tape, similar to a child's mittens, so that they may be worn around the neck, always handy for use (Fig. 3-3).

In my own collection, flat padded potholders are in the majority, although there is a tremendous variety within that category. Carole Austin gave me a rectangular white potholder, machine-quilted in a random grid and edged with white rickrack, starched and ironed to perfection. Bets Ramsey endowed an old nine-patch square with new life by backing it with faded, soft denim and then machine quilting it (Fig. 3-4). In a workshop where I had asked participants to bring in scraps of trims, one student wove a variety of tapes, using both the right and wrong sides, to produce a striking potholder (Fig. 3-5).

Fig. 3-3.
This pair of potholders can be worn around one's neck.

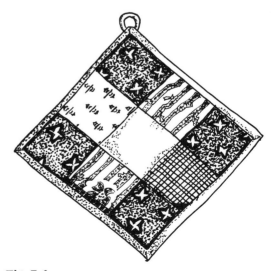

Fig. 3-4.
Even the pieces are pieced in this old quilt square, made into a potholder by Bets Ramsey.

Fig. 3-5.
This potholder is woven of decorative trims and tapes.

Proving that potholders can evoke humor, a commercially produced one of white fabric bound in red proclaims in red letters, "Cleanliness is next to impossible."

Knitted, Crocheted, Woven, Slipcovered

Most knitted potholders fit within the flat category. Denying the above proclamation that "Cleanliness is next to impossible," two pristine, white cotton, knitted potholders made in Denmark by the mother of Betty Stuntz conjure up visions of an immaculate kitchen and a very ladylike cook. Surviving from early in the twentieth century—and obviously never used—they remain virginally spotless and dainty.

Perhaps they were used, as Susan Swan suggests in *Plain and Fancy: American Women and Their Needlework 1700 to 1850*, only on special occasions to lift a teapot at a social event (Fig. 3-6).

The Oakland Museum owns an unusual knitted potholder of red-and-white wool that goes beyond the flat format (Fig. 3-7). Made as a tiny pocket, 2" by 4", it must have had a twin, with both slipping over the handles of a soup pot; since it sports decorative dangling pompons, maybe the pockets were placed over the heat-conductive handles of a silver tray or other hot serving dish.

Judging from the collections I have seen, crocheted potholders far outnumber knitted ones. They blossomed during the 1930s and 1940s, disguised as doll dresses, bloomers, acorns, and animals (Fig. 3-8). The American Thread Company published booklets of potholder designs accompanied by appropriate recipes, such as a bumblebee potholder with a recipe for honey date

Fig. 3-6.
Special hot pads were saved for use at social occasions, such as ladies' tea parties.

Fig. 3-7.
This tiny knitted potholder may have joined a twin to carry a silver tray. Collection Oakland Museum.

sticks. Countless geometric variations—circles, squares, hexagons—grew in the color combinations popular in kitchens of that time. Red and white and green and white seem to have been the favorites.

Surely, a one-of-a-kind example is the red-and-white hot pad owned by Eli Leon (Fig. 3-9). I call it "Poor Pitiful

Fig. 3-8.
Crocheted potholders often took the form of clothing. Author's collection.

Fig. 3-9.
This red-and-white crocheted potholder depicts a sad-faced doll. Collection Eli Leon.

Pearl'' after a mournful little doll I remember from years past. Eli found the potholder at a California flea market, and its appealing sad smile must have saved it from the stove's cruel heat. Two cotton string crochet ovals form the body and head, with pantaloons and feet completing the 9½″ doll shape. One wonders if it started as a circular potholder and grew into a doll or if it was meant to be as it is.

Crochet's popularity continued into the 1950s, when J. and P. Coates-Clark published a "pot-holder-of-the-month" booklet that included instructions for such wonders as umbrella, Easter egg, ship's wheel, penguin, snowman, and Christmas tree potholders (Fig. 3-10). Most of these were made with stringlike cotton threads, such as Knit-cro-sheen. Another publication featured a red-and-white sugar and creamer pair of potholders (Fig. 3-11). All these cunning crochet hot pads were among those that cooks refrained from subjecting to the hazards of the stove, as evidenced by the vast numbers of them that have survived.

Potholders surely made for short-term use are those woven of fresh palm fronds. As recently as 1980, these were in common use by peasants in Panama. One assumes that they would have to be discarded when the leaves dry, but the raw material is cheap and plentiful for making new ones.

My favorite potholder for hard use is the woven cotton looper variety made by my daughters in the 1960s (Fig. 3-12). Looms and loopers are available and children are still making looper potholders. In 1992, *Handwoven* magazine published the results of The Great Jersey Loop Caper, an appeal from editor Linda Ligon for children to send to the magazine their efforts at woven looper potholders. More than 1,200 were submitted, and the ripples of interest spread far beyond the original project. The most ambitious undertaking was a huge wall hanging of woven potholders assembled by children in the classes of New Orleans teacher Roseline Young.

Be sure you buy cotton loopers and not nylon ones, which are not heatproof and often will not stretch to fit the loom. (See the Appendix for sources for cotton loopers and looms.)

Fig. 3-10.
These potholders were designed for each month. You can guess which months these depict.

Fig. 3-11.
These hot pads represent a red-and-white sugar and creamer. Author's collection.

Fig. 3-12.
Loom-woven cotton looper potholders are still a favorite.

Perfect size, flexibility, and insulation, as well as pleasing colors and designs, add up to make the ideal potholder. I like them so much that I have been known to reupholster them when they wear thin! I thought that I was the only eccentric in the world who did this, but I have found at least two other potholder people who do. Ann DeWitt sent me a bedraggled and burnt potholder with a note attached saying that it obviously needed a new cover. Jane McElroy has been known to recover old ones several times. She says, "They have such a life to them, it's hard for me to throw them away."

Practicality rather than sentimentality dicates another flat potholder, a slipcovered one of a pair owned by Beryl Self (Fig. 3-13). A thick, padded core and a removable cotton fabric cover permit easy washing and quick

Fig. 3-13.
A slipcoverd potholder is easy to launder. Collection Beryl Self.

drying. Also, there is a magnet sewn onto the core, providing a practical solution by hanging the potholder from a metal surface, such as the oven door or the refrigerator.

Puppets, Mitts, Sleeves

Perhaps even more practical than flat potholders, mitts give allover protection because they cover the entire hand. (At the turn of the century, English country folk called hot mitts "kettle gloves.") Shaped like a mitten, though sometimes without a thumb, many commercially made ones are elaborate, masked as birds, frogs, or other creatures. With ears, wings, feathers, and gaping mouths, they often live a double life as puppets for creative children. (See color section.)

Even more protection is provided by a double mitt, which is ideal for lifting a steaming casserole from the oven. An oblong padded shape with a pocket at either end, the double mitt shelters both hands without the necessity of two separate potholders (Fig. 3-14). In a Cleveland, Ohio, family in the 1930s, their double mitt was called a "long John."

Sleeves, or panhandlers, are specialized potholders. Tailored to fit

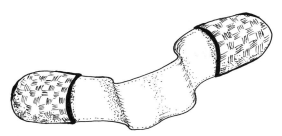

Fig. 3-14.
The family of Wilhelmina Littleton Sullivan called their double mitt a "long John."

snugly over the handle of a pan, it is used on iron skillets and on many of the newer gourmet cooking utensils. There is little surface for decoration, but Vicki Johnson fashioned colorful ones from fine Seminole patchwork (Fig. 3-15).

Everyone has his or her favorite kind of potholder, whether to make or to use or to simply own. Many collect potholders that they never use. Their collections may be comprehensive, in-

cluding all forms and techniques, or as specialized as one I heard of that contained only those potholders depicting undergarments—panties, bras, long underwear, and a corset. Some collections might include potholder holders, such as the basket pictured (Fig. 3-16). Baskets were usually made as a set with potholders to match. Other collections might include only potholders paired with companion decorative aprons, such as a strawberry potholder and an apron with a strawberry pocket (Fig. 3-17) or a football potholder Velcro-attached to an apron printed to resemble your favorite football team's uniform (Fig. 3-18).

Fig. 3-16.
This embroidered basket for holding potholders probably had its own matching potholders at one time, though we have tucked looper ones in for the photograph.

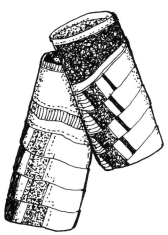

Fig. 3-15.
These are Vicki Johnson's Seminole patchwork sleeve-type hot-pot holders.

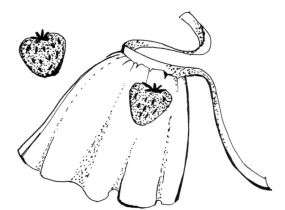

Fig. 3-17.
A strawberry hot pad matches the pocket of a
companion apron.

You may be a collector, too, even
though you've never consciously sought
potholders. Since a collection is a group
of objects accumulated in one location,
almost anyone who has a kitchen and
who cooks has a potholder collection or,
at least, a head start at one. Whether
you use yours or collect for the fun of
it, exploring the vast variety of potholders provides an enjoyable challenge.

Fig. 3-18.
This barbeque chef wears an apron for his favorite football team. His hot mitt looks like a football
and, when not in use, hangs from the apron by a
patch of Velcro.

4

Making Potholders

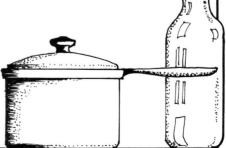

Potholders are made for use, and in that process, they get splashed, spotted, stained, scorched, burned, and simply worn out. Since their usual life expectancy is short and their role is played in the privacy of the kitchen, time spent in making potholders should be minimal—if you invest too much time, you may hesitate to use them—though a humorous or attractive potholder will certainly enliven a humdrum chore. If you are making them as a gift or strictly as a decorative item, however, you may want to work more thoughtfully and carefully in choosing particular colors and designs.

Choosing the Right Materials

If a potholder is eventually to fill its normal role of handling hot items, care must be given in selecting the materials. Sturdy cottons are best for the outer fabric, though blends are acceptable. Common sense tells us to avoid sheer or fragile fabrics. You probably have a treasure house of items in your closets that will stimulate spontaneous and lively results: half-finished quilt blocks, trials that were the wrong color, bits and pieces left over from quilts or stitcheries or garments, whole works that were unsuccessful or never to be completed (be prepared to cut these up), tail ends of Seminole patchwork, short ends of bias tape, rickrack, and other trims (Fig. 4-1). Working with these expendable goods encourages a feeling of freedom in the creative process. Binding and backing fabrics are most practical in dark colors, which set

Fig. 4-1.
Fragments of patchwork and trims encourage inventive design solutions.

off the artwork of the front of the potholder while also showing less soil and scorch (Fig. 4-2).

New miracle products are coming on the market all the time. A recent one is paper backed fusible web, a real boon to appliqué. There are several brands, among them Wonder-Under, Magic Fuse, Trans Web, HeatnBond, and Aleene's Hot Stitch Fusible Web. Use any of these when paper backed fusible web is called for. It will make your life much easier, first by stabilizing the appliqué fabric for easier cutting, and then by adhering the appliqué shape to the background. It may be bonded by heat or re-inforced by stitching. Be sure to follow the manufacturer's instructions.

For filler or insulation most potholder makers prefer natural fiber: layers of worn toweling or jeans denim or squares cut from old cotton mattress pads (Fig. 4-3). Cotton batting is another option. (I tried to get information about the relative merits of natural fibers compared with synthetics such as polyester as to insulating qualities, flammability, and heat resistance, but was unable to get these facts.) If you are reaching the bottom of the barrel of scraps for filler, piece bits together.

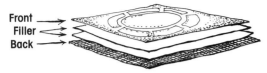

Fig. 4-2.
The layers of a potholder consist of the front or top, the filler, and the back.

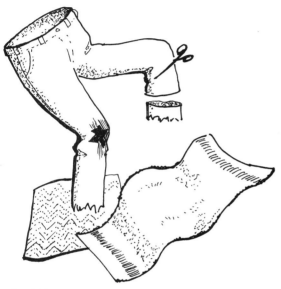

Fig. 4-3.
Worn blue jeans, old towels, and cotton mattress pads make excellent filler for hot pads.

Just butt them together and zigzag with your machine or whip by hand with really big stitches. This will not show in the finished product and machine quilting through outer layers will hold it in permanent place. Avoid using so much filler, though, that your potholder loses its flexibility. Two filler layers of toweling or denim are sufficient while one layer of toweling with one layer of quilt batting (preferably cotton) might show quilting to better advantage.

Table felt, purchased at fabric stores, is a possible filler if you prefer not to use recycled materials. The table felt that I found was 100% cotton. To preshrink it, which is vital, I first zigzagged the cut edges to prevent raveling and then threw it in my washer and dryer at the temperatures I normally use. The table felt shrank about 4″ per yard in length and somewhat less in width.

There are several varieties of heat-reflective fabrics, some quilted and some not, often used for ironing board covers. These may serve as the outer "hot" side of your potholder; if you find the color and texture less than pleasing, as I do, bury them within the potholder.

In several potholders, I have specified prequilted fabric or felt. Fabric trends are as fickle as fashion, so you may not find what you want when you want it. The fiber content of my scrap felt was cotton or wool, but shops today feature acrylic felt. Prequilted fabric comes with the outer layer in cotton/poly blends, as well as 100% cotton, and the filler is polyester. Be sure that if you can't get what you want, you at least are aware of what you are getting.

Suggestions for Decorative Tops

Now for the fun part—the decorative top or front. With your scrap treasures at hand, create with abandon by cutting, adding to, turning at odd angles, or even trying startling color combinations. Think "Quick!" "Spontaneous!" You've nothing to lose. If you sew at all, you probably already have everything you need. In making the potholders for this book, I used only materials at hand, except for the table felt, which I wanted to try as a filler.

If there ever was a time to eschew hand work and take advantage of your sewing machine, this is it. The most basic straight-stitch machine is adequate, though zigzag and ornamental stitches give a broader range of quick effects. However, if you prefer hand sewing, you should be able to adapt the instructions to your use, too.

Potholders also offer an opportunity for inventiveness in technique. So far, no one has set up rules—that is, judging criteria—and let's hope no one does. Though I will show you some possible methods of construction, I hope you will invent your own. As long as you keep function in mind, anything is acceptable. Just be sure that your materials are appropriate, your insulation is sufficient, and your shape is compact, with no dangling or jutting appendages.

Determine the size you want your potholder to be. A diameter of 5½″ to 6½″ makes an easily handled potholder. A larger size is tempting because it provides more space for inventive design, but it is sometimes awkward to use. Still, the larger size, 9″ or so, may serve as a hot mat protecting the table surface from an oven-hot casserole.

You may make the top separately or work directly on a layer of filler. The latter method gives a foundation on which you can lay shapes for machine piecing or machine appliqué.

I have sometimes picked up scraps from my workroom floor and composed a hot-pad top with them. Since this proved so successful, I now keep a basket near my cutting space and brush the scraps off into the basket to save until it's potholder-making time. These odd shapes are often the basis for an unusual design. (See color section.)

At other times, I work in the traditional patchwork technique, seaming pieces together, but I also leave cloth edges raw, overlapping them and then securing them with several rows of straight stitching in contrasting thread colors. As well as fastening the edge down, this stitching becomes a drawing line, enhancing the design. I may prepiece or stitch the pieces directly onto the filler fabric, perhaps using a stitch-and-press technique (Fig. 4-4).

One of my favorite scrap items is Seminole patchwork. For the uninitiated, Seminole patchwork is a machine-worked method of making the intricate pieced bands that are an integral part of the costume of the Seminole Indians of Florida (Fig. 4-5) Entire books have been devoted to this technique; if you're not familiar with it, I suggest you check your local library or bookstore. In addition, see the Appendix. A finished result requires a certain amount of accuracy and skill. Since I am neither mathematical nor precision-oriented, I always have bits left over; they are elegant beginnings for a hot-pad top. I add borders in compatible colors or turn the Seminole on an angle and add triangles to reach the desired size and shape. A squiggle of rickrack adds dash. In one instance, I combined Seminole with a piece of folk embroidery from a Mexican garment. Rather than lose the zigzag edges of the Semi-

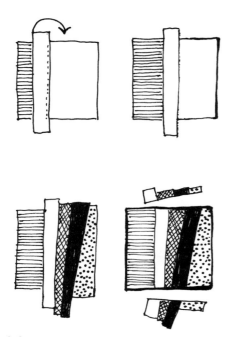

Fig. 4-4.
The stitch-and-press technique lays strips of fabric directly on the filler. Beginning at top left in this drawing, stitch two pieces, right sides together, then flip the top piece to the right. Lay a third piece, right side down on top of previous piece, stitch, and flip. Continue until the filler is covered. Trim edges.

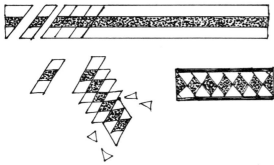

Fig. 4-5.
In Seminole piecing, long strips of fabric are sewn together, cut into pieces, then resewn in new arrangements. Variations are endless.

nole patchwork in a seam, I machine appliquéd it with several rows of straight stitches along the stair-step edges. (See color section.)

Occasionally, most of us undertake ambitious pieces that don't work out as planned. These failures can become a potholder bonanza if you have the courage to cut them into hot-pad-size pieces. When you do this, you see the colors and shapes with a fresh eye, enabling you to choose what is needed to make them work as a handsome potholder. Perhaps all that's necessary is binding and a loop, or you may want to add some machine appliqué or bright stitching for emphasis. (See color section.)

Quilt squares worked as samples or those worked in colors that didn't fit in with the rest of the quilt or old quilt squares need only a harmonizing binding and a few quilting lines to become collectors' items or gifts treasured by a friend.

The appealing motif of a print fabric can be highlighted with quilting and then backed and bound in a companion color to form an easy potholder. At an estate sale, I found a veritable treasure of unusual fabrics printed with the labels of canned foods, seed packets, and beer brands, which I fashioned into potholders in only minutes using this method. (See color section.)

Colleen Williams devised another simple but effective decorative technique in a Christmas potholder for Joy Swift. Colleen layered red fabric, filler, and green fabric and then machine quilted with red thread. Starting at the center with a star, she continued spiraling out, following the contours of the star. Red binding and a loop finished the piece (Fig. 4-6).

I have already mentioned using worn denim jeans as filler. If you like the subtlety of color obtained by ripping out a faded seam or a hem or by saving the "crumpled" look of a drawstring casing, denim also holds many decorative possibilities. You might even incorporate a label or a pocket from the denim garment (Fig. 4-7). Nancy Welch wove denim strips mixed with other colorful fabric strips for a sturdy "rag rug" potholder.

Fabric crayons, available from art stores, offer another decorative option, or you may use ordinary wax crayons and heat-set them with your iron. However, make sure you protect the surface of your iron and your ironing board

Fig. 4-7.
This denim potholder exploits the subtleties of worn creases and a crumpled drawstring casing. A jeans label is added.

from the waxy color by laying cotton fabric over the ironing board surface and between the iron and the drawing. Draw on white or pale colors of cotton fabric, filling lots of the color area for the strongest visual effect. This is a great medium for children. Katrina Shipley, who had used this technique with her preschoolers, adopted their naive style to make a housewarming gift for her mother-in-law, Pat Shipley (Fig. 4-8).

Letting your imagination run free conjures up all sorts of representational possibilities, such as fried eggs with a strip of bacon or a piece of pie or cake (Fig. 4-9), the palm of a hand, a face, a strawberry, or a house. (See color section.) These could be appliquéd by hand or by machine, painted with textile

Fig. 4-6.
A simple quilted Christmas star makes a striking hot-pot holder. Colleen Williams for Joy Swift.

Fig. 4-8.
A wax-crayon drawing bids a warm welcome to a new home. Katrina Shipley for Pat Shipley.

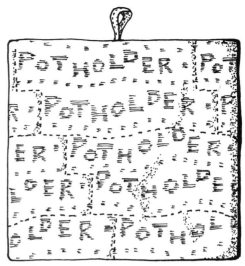

Fig. 4-10.
Rubber-stamped letters proclaim this item's identity.

paints, or pieced, depending on your talents, time, and the subject matter.

A collection of rubber stamps suggests countless combinations for printed tops (Fig. 4-10), using indelible inks, of course, since laundering is a likelihood. Here's a hint for the remedy to a less-than-perfect imprint: touch it up with an extra-fine-point Sharpie pen in the

appropriate color. I find these pens invaluable for all sorts of touch-ups, such as a stitch that shows on a dark background when I don't want it to. Color the stitches with a Sharpie the color of the background fabric.

If you are skilled at batik or silk-screen printing, use these techniques for unique hot-pot holders. One of the

Fig. 4-9.
Here are some mouth-watering possibilities for decorative potholders.

easiest and most effective ways of printing your own decorative tops is by potato printing using Versatex, Createx, or other water-soluble textile paint. (See the Appendix for supply sources.)

While decorative tops exercise your creative capacities, they still must be backed by strong, functional methods of construction.

Construction Methods for Flat Potholders

Pillow Slip

The pillow-slip method is also appropriate for shapes other than square, such as round, free-form, hexagonal, and so on.

1. Do decorative work for the top or front of your potholder.

2. Pin the decorative top together with filler layer(s).

3. Machine (or hand) quilt through top and filler. Stop all quilting at least ¼″ from edges of decorative top.

4. Trim filler ¼″ smaller than top on all sides to eliminate bulk in the seams.

5. Cut backing same size as top.

6. Make a loop for hanging, using bias tape stitched along its length, or a sturdy cord. The tape or cord should be about 3½″ to 4″ long, giving a loop of approximately 1¼″ to 1¾″.

7. Pin the top piece and backing right sides together, pinning the loop inside a corner (Fig. 4-11).

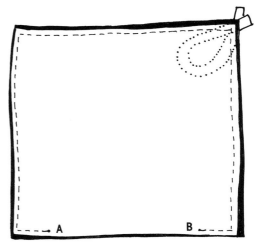

Fig. 4-11.
With the top piece and backing right sides together, pin the loop inside a corner. Stitch from A to B the long way, leaving one side open, as shown.

8. (See Fig. 4-11.) Starting ½″ from corner (A), stitch a few stitches, backstitch, and continue toward the corner, making a ¼″ seam. Continue stitching the other three sides and ½″ on the original side (B). Backstitch at the end. Trim corners.

9. Turn right side out. Pin fourth side, turning raw edges in, and topstitch or whip by hand.

10. Additional quilting may be done at this time.

Mitered Corner

1. Do decorative work for top of potholder. Trim to desired size.

2. Cut filler slightly larger than top to allow for quilting distortion.

3. Cut backing fabric 1½″ larger than top on all sides (Fig. 4-12a).

4. With back wrong side up, pin all layers securely and machine quilt. Trim filler edges to match top edges. Trim backing to 1″ from top edges (Fig. 4-12b).

5. To miter corners, fold potholder on diagonal with top up, as shown, and stitch corners of backing at right angle to the fold, about ⅜″, (Fig. 4-12c). Backstitch over stitches to secure. Refold diagonally to other corners, stitch, and trim all four corners.

6. Fold backing fabric to front. Poke corners with a sharp instrument. Turn edges under, pin, and topstitch. If you have left too wide a margin of fabric to fold under neatly, trim edges before pinning and stitching.

7. Loop may be stitched to the back of a corner or a plastic ring may be sewn on.

Bias Binding Method

The bias-binding method is also appropriate for shapes other than squares. For better flow of the binding, round the corners of square pieces.

1. Do decorative work for top, then layer with filler and backing that is cut to approximately same size as top. Pin securely and quilt.

2. Trim top, filler, and backing edges to same size.

3. Measure 1½″-wide bias strip long enough to go around potholder plus 5″.

4. With right sides of potholder and bias strip together, beginning at a corner, stitch around edge making ¼″ seam (Fig. 4-13a).

5. When you reach the final corner, fold out beginning bias and stitch up to the fold (Fig. 4-13b).

6. Trim corners, if you have not already rounded them.

7. Turn bias to back, folding edge under. Pin in place, covering stitching just done. Also fold in edges of 5″ tab and pin (Fig. 4-13c)

8. On front of potholder, stitch in the ditch, pulling pins out just ahead of machine foot. Continue stitching onto tab. ("Stitch in the ditch" means to sew in the seam so that the stitching hardly shows, Fig. 4-14). If you have pinned as directed, stitching should catch the binding on the back.

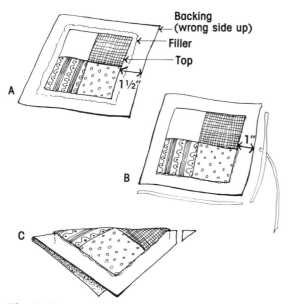

Fig. 4-12.
Mitered corner method.

Backing (wrong side up)
Filler
Top
1½″

A

1″

B

C

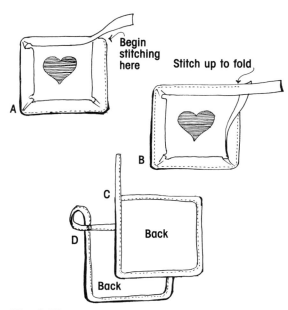

Begin stitching here

Stitch up to fold

A

B

C

D

Back

Back

Fig. 4-13.
Bias-binding method.

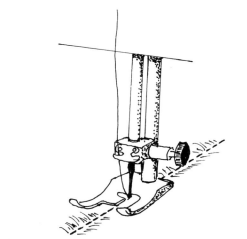

Fig. 4-14.
Stitch in the ditch.

9. Fold tab back onto potholder and stitch for loop (Fig. 4-13d).

Tape Binding with Mitered Corners

1. Do decorative work for top, then layer with filler and backing, all cut to the same size. Pin securely and quilt. Leave the corners square.

2. With right sides together, start sewing binding tape, either bias or straight grain, along one side, not in a corner. Fold end of tape under, (Fig. 4-15a).

3. As you stitch right side of tape to the right side of the potholder, stitch to a point just short of ¼″ of the corner. Then turn potholder and stitch off the edge along which you have been sewing, forming a right angle of stitches (see Fig. 4-15a).

4. Remove potholder from sewing machine and fold tape, (Fig. 4-15b and c). Pin in place and stitch along next side, making ¼″ seam. Continue, repeating the process at each corner.

5. End of tape should overlap beginning fold by about ¼″.

6. Fold to back of potholder, pinning tape, including miters, in place on back side, and pin and stitch in the ditch from the front, as in the bias-binding method.

7. Attach a plastic ring or separate tape tab for hanging.

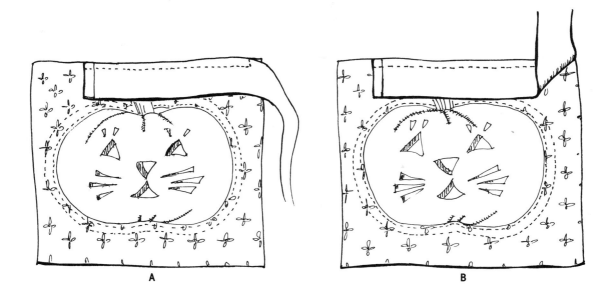

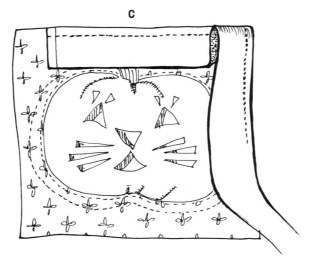

Fig. 4-15.
Tape binding with mitered corners.

Free and Easy

This method will work for any shape.

1. Make decorative top and layer with filler and backing cut to approximately same size as the top. Pin and machine quilt.

2. Trim edges and stay-stitch with a straight stitch.

3. Leave edges raw, controlled only by wide zigzag stitch. This looks more finished if you work the zigzag over a cord such as number 8 pearl cotton and shorten the stitch length to form a satin stitch (Fig. 4-16). Another way of avoiding an edge that ripples is using a water-soluble stabilizer. There are several on the market. Lay the stabilizer

over or under the edge to be stitched, then stitch with a zigzag stitch, and tear away excess stabilizer. Any remaining stabilizer can be washed away with cold water. If you have a serger, use a short, balanced stitch at the edge.

4. Add loop, if desired.

This method works well without filler if you use two thick layers of cotton fabric, such as Haitian cotton, which is a nubby upholstery fabric. I machine appliquéd scraps of bright-colored, lightweight cotton fabrics in a random pattern on the surface for embellishment when I tried this.

Easy Felt Construction

Since felt is a nonwoven fabric and doesn't ravel, it is ideal for youngsters to work with. Washing is chancy, though I have done it by using cold water and by line drying.

1. Cut two 6″ squares and one 5½″ square of ordinary felt (available in fabric and hobby stores).

2. Cut simple felt shapes to decorate one of the 6″ squares.

3. Stitch these on with a running stitch by hand or machine. A French knot may be sufficient to hold smaller shapes.

4. Sandwich the smaller square between the two larger ones, right sides out (Fig. 4-17), and stitch around the edge with straight stitch or an open zigzag stitch.

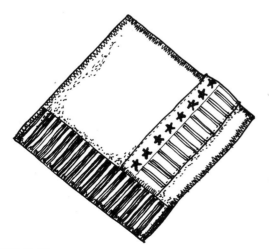

Fig. 4-16.
This potholder is made of denim and decorative trim. The raw edge is finished with a zigzag stitch over cord in the Free and Easy method.

Potholder projects.

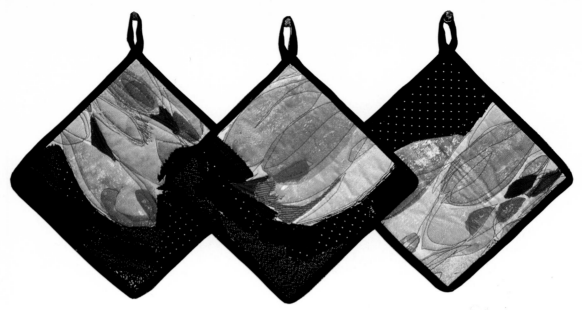

An unsuccessful potato print of leaping flames was cut apart and reworked to form potholders.

A simplified drawing of a friend's new house inspired this gift potholder.

Benjamin and Jacob Vander Plas transform hot mitts into handpuppets.

Laotian potholder becomes a case for your sunglasses.

This gift potholder repeats the colors and motifs of a wedding invitation.

Feathers found on the beach were laid on blue print fabric for this print by Pat Shipley.

"Ultimate" potholder won a blue ribbon and prize tray at the county fair.

A small, soft potholder becomes a needle case.

Potholder wheels snap onto a 1920s auto which has been incorporated into an assemblage by Ray Ward. The word "holders" does not apply just to pots, but to irons and other hot implements as well. Photo by Brant Ward.

Bits of Seminole patchwork combined with Mexican embroidery and rainbow colors.

Quick potholders made from printed fabrics resembling labels.

Joan Schulze carved a rubber eraser to stamp her smiling sun.

Crocheted potholders transform a simple blue vest. Courtesy of Bonnie Stone.

A Garibaldi fish swims amid cool waters and strands of kelp on this potholder by Vicki Johnson.

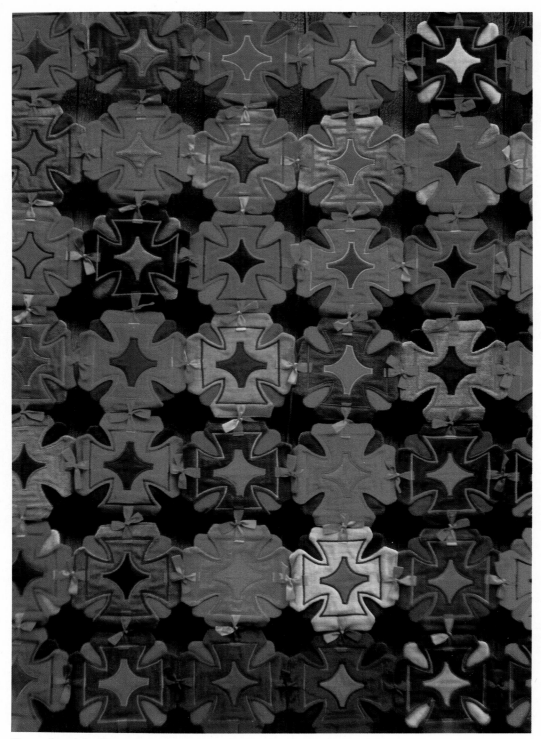

Nancy Gano's brilliant space divider is made of potholder units tied together.

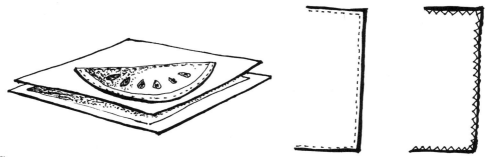

Fig. 4-17.
One layer of felt is sufficient filler for a felt potholder, which may be stitched with a straight or a zigzag stitch.

Slipcover Construction

1. Cut table felt or other padding in a 6″ square.

2. Secure a small magnet to padding by stitching a square of lightweight fabric over it (Fig. 4-18a). Packages of magnets are available in craft or hardware stores. You may need two magnets if your potholder is heavy.

3. Cut one 6¾″ square of cotton fabric. This is the surface to be decorated. It

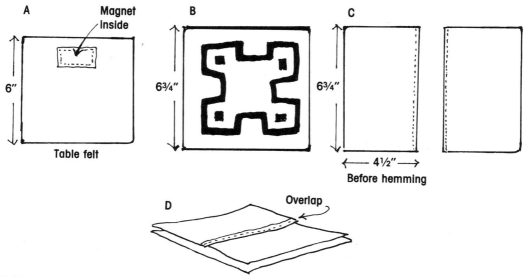

Fig. 4-18.
Slipcover construction.

could be painted, printed, appliquéd, or pieced in a patchwork square (Fig. 4-18b).

4. Cut two pieces 6¾″ by 4½″ of any compatible cotton fabric (Fig. 4-18c).

5. Make a tiny hem along one long side of each of the latter two pieces.

6. Right sides together, with the outer raw edges matching, pin decorated square and two hemmed pieces in place. The hemmed edges will overlap at center (Fig. 4-18d).

7. Stitch around outer edge of square, making ¼″ seams. Trim corners.

8. Turn right-side-out and slip padding inside.

Janie's Method

I have saved the best of the flat potholders till last. Janie Warnick, whose brain I equate with a computer—only Janie is more creative—has devised the following method. Janie mass-produces potholders for fund-raising events and has honed her methods and skills to

produce an attractive product in a minimum of time. I will give instructions for making a flat potholder, followed by Janie's hints for mass production. Although she gives instructions for a circular hot pad, this method is appropriate for other shapes as well. (Janie is co-author of *Gifts Galore*.)

1. Cut two circles 6″ or 7″ in diameter from prequilted fabric.

2. Cut a slit about 3″ long in the center of one circle. Cut on the straight grain of the fabric (Fig. 4-19a).

3. Cut a 4″ piece of single- or double-fold bias tape and stitch the length of the open side to close it. (If yours came flat, fold it in half and stitch.)

4. With right sides together and bias tape folded to form a loop pinned between the two layers, stitch all the way around the circle with generous ⅛″ seam (Fig. 4-19b).

5. Turn right side out through slit.

6. Run a pointed instrument all along the seam. Press and topstitch ⅛″ from the edge with a straight stitch.

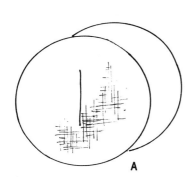 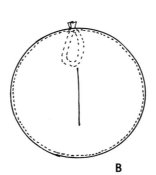 

| A | B | C |

Fig. 4-19.
Janie's method.

7. With paper-backed fusible web bonded to the back of fabric you have chosen for appliqué, cut a simple shape. Janie suggests cookie cutters as patterns, which may be traced on the paper side of the bonded fabric.

8. Bond the appliqué shape to cover the slit and stitch around the shape with a satin stitch to finish. This closes the opening and also quilts the potholder (Fig. 4-19c).

To facilitate quantity construction, Janie stacks the prequilted fabrics and, using a salad plate or a fruit bowl as a template, cuts with her rotary cutter. She stitches the entire length of a package of bias tape and cuts this into 4″ lengths. She stacks these prefab pieces at her sewing machine and flies into production.

Her creative mind has conjured up numerous variations, but my favorite was adding a heart-shaped pocket to the potholder and tucking a choice recipe on a decorative card into the pocket. Janie says these were supersellers at her school bazaar (Fig. 4-20).

She suggests covering the slit, as described above, with a small heart, using two or three rows of straight stitch rather than satin stitch (Fig. 4-21a). Then make a pocket in the following manner: Cut a heart pattern about 4″ at its widest. Cut two pieces of cotton print, right sides together, using the heart pattern. Stitch around the heart, leaving an opening for turning along one lower side. Turn to the right side and press. You will stitch the turning opening as you straight stitch the pocket over the smaller heart (Fig. 4-21b). Be sure to leave the pocket open at the top (Fig. 4-21c), and tuck in your recipe card.

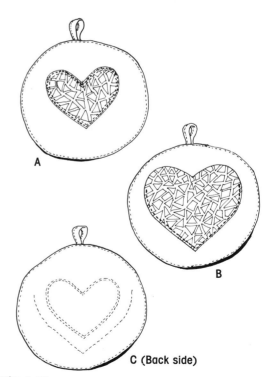

Fig. 4-20.
A favorite recipe is tucked into a potholder pocket.

Fig. 4-21.
Making Janie's pocket potholder.

Construction Methods for Dimensional Potholders

Mitt Construction

The simplest mitt takes the form of an arch or of a child's mitten (Fig. 4-22). Any decoration or quilting should take place before the pattern pieces are cut.

1. Trace the pattern on fabric, decorate it, then quilt it. Before cutting, lay pattern over it again to check accuracy. Cut two quilted pieces for either the arch or the mitten. Use Fig. 4-23 for a pattern, blowing it up as large as you want.

2. Placing right sides together, sew the quilted pieces together, leaving the wrist open. Turn right side out.

3. Bind the opening with bias binding, making a loop for hanging.

Open-Mouth Mitt Construction

1. Cut two of piece A and one of piece B from prequilted fabric. (See Fig. 4-24.)

2. Right sides together, sew A pieces along sides for 6½", making ⅜" seams. (See Fig. 4-25).

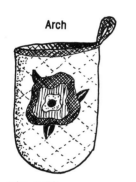
Arch

Mitten

Fig. 4-22.
The simplest mitt potholders, an arch and a mitten.

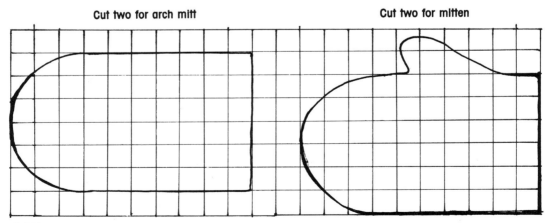

Cut two for arch mitt

Cut two for mitten

Fig. 4-23.
Patterns for two simple mitts. Each square equals 1″.

MAKING POTHOLDERS

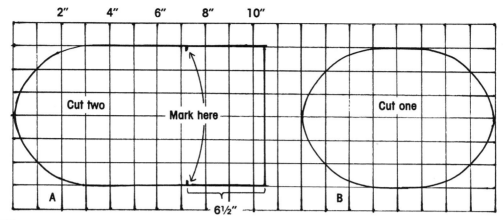

Fig. 4-24.
Pattern for puppet mitts. Each square equals 1″.

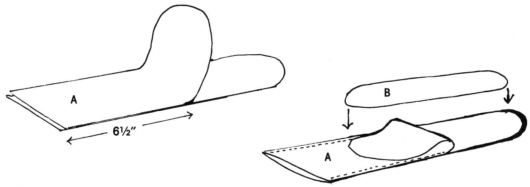

Fig. 4-25.
Assembly of puppet mitt.

3. Right sides together, sew piece B to A pieces, matching arches, with ⅜″ seams. (See Fig. 4-25).

4. Turn right side out. If you are making a puppet creature, a tiny stitch pinching the corners of the mouth together should aid in giving the mouth form (Fig. 4-26).

5. Bind the opening with bias binding, forming a loop for hanging.

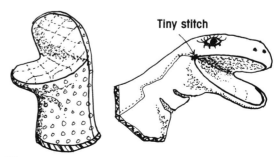

Fig. 4-26.
Puppet-type potholders.

Diagonal Pocket Mitt

This piece is constructed to be used as a flat potholder or as a mitt.

1. Cut two of piece A (Fig. 4-27).

2. Cut filler ¼″ smaller all around than piece A.

3. Place filler between A pieces with their right sides out and machine quilt.

4. Cut one piece B (Fig. 4-27). Make sure the diagonal cut is wider than your hand since this forms the pocket opening.

5. With bias or straight-grain fabric, bind the diagonal edge of piece B.

6. Lay piece B on top of quilted square and stitch around outer edge.

7. Bind the outer edge with bias binding, forming a loop for hanging (Fig.

4-27c), or finish as in the Free and Easy method, zigzagging the edge over number 8 pearl cotton.

Double Mitt Construction

Double mitts vary in length, from 20″ to 28″. Here is a pattern that you may adapt to your preference. (See Fig. 4-28.) Piece A must be padded. The smaller pockets (piece B) need not be padded.

1. With prequilted fabric folded double, lay pattern piece A (Fig. 4-28a) so that straight side is on fold. Cut around the other sides. When unfolded, the shape should resemble Fig. 4-28b without the pockets.

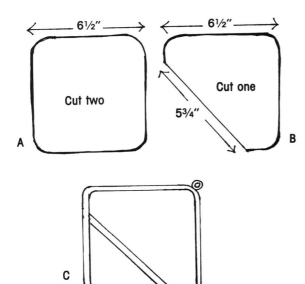

Fig. 4-27.
Diagonal pocket mitt.

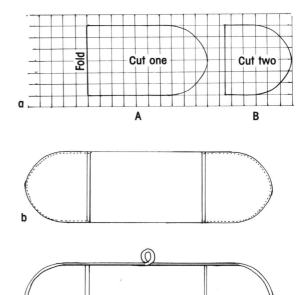

Fig. 4-28.
Double mitt. Each square equals 1″.

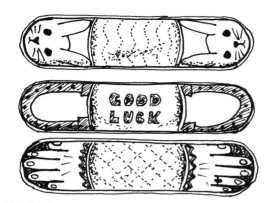

Fig. 4-29.
Double mitts need not be plain.

Double mitts I have seen are usually of plain or printed fabric, with the bias binding as the only trim. There's no reason you cannot use the surface for creative printing, painting, appliqué, or stitchery. Here are some ideas (Fig. 4-29).

Sleeve or Panhandler Construction

1. Measure around the pan's handle at the largest point and add 1″. This is side A (Fig. 4-30a).

2. Side B is the length of the handle plus ¼″ (Fig. 4-30b).

3. Cut one piece, using these measurements, from prequilted material (Fig. 4-30c).

4. Cut bias binding to equal side A plus 3½″.

5. Bind side A. A long tail of binding will remain unattached (Fig. 4-30c).

2. Cut two of piece B and bind the straight edge of each with bias binding.

3. With right sides out, place pockets at ends of piece A. Pin in place and stitch (Fig. 4-28b).

4. Sew bias binding around edge of entire mitt, making a loop for hanging (Fig. 4-28c).

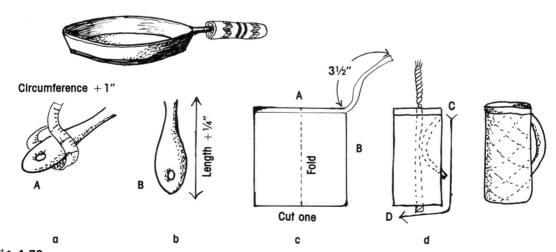

Fig. 4-30.
Sleeve construction.

6. Fold on dotted line, right sides together, with a strong cord pinned inside as shown. This will facilitate turning later (Fig. 4-30d).

7. Tuck loose tail of binding inside and insert end into seam (Fig. 4-30d). Pin in place.

8. Stitch from C to D, making a ¼" seam (Fig. 4-30d).

9. Turn right side out by pulling tail of cord. Trim cord carefully from seam.

Alternate Sleeve Construction

1. Measure width of pan's handle and add ½". This is the short side (Fig. 4-31a).

2. Measure length of handle and double it. This is the long side (see Fig. 4-31a).

3. Cut one thickness of toweling to these measurements. If handle is unusually thick, allow for this in your measurements by adding ½" to each measurement.

4. Cut outer fabric 2" longer than toweling and wide enough so that when folded over toweling, the two sides will overlap (Fig. 4-31b).

5. Fold in ends and then sides, as if wrapping a package (Fig. 4-31c).

6. Pin in place and stitch, as shown.

7. Quilt at this time, if desired.

8. Fold in half crosswise, right sides out. If hanging loop is required, insert

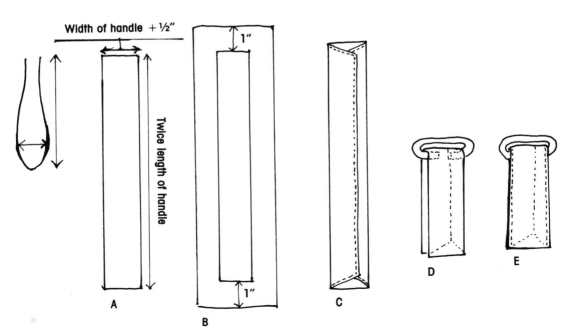

Fig. 4-31.
Alternate sleeve construction.

bias tape (that has been stitched lengthwise) at either side of fold (Fig. 4-31d).

9. Stitch the sides with least seam possible—about ⅛" (Fig. 4-31e).

Another Sleeve Construction Method

1. Measure around the pan's handle at the largest point and add ¾". This is side A (Fig. 4-32a).

2. Measure length of handle and add ½". This is side B (Fig. 4-32b).

3. Using these measurements, cut one piece of prequilted fabric (Fig. 4-32c).

4. Turn up ½" hem on one side of A (Fig. 4-32d).

5. Fold on fold line, right sides out, and pin.

6. Trim corners (Fig. 4-32e).

7. Insert hanging loop of bias tape at any point.

8. Stitch from C to D with a wide zigzag or serger stitch (Fig. 4-32f).

Cutting Your Own Bias Binding

You may want to make your own bias binding of a print fabric or for a precise color match. If you are making only enough for one potholder, lay a straight edge at a 45° angle to the selvage and cut with a rotary cutter. Move straight edge 1½", parallel to the first cut, and cut again (Fig. 4-33a). If you do not have a rotary cutter, mark the lines with a soft pencil or a ballpoint pen and cut with your trusty sharp scissors. If you have to piece the bias

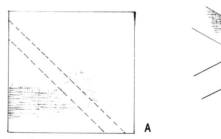

Fig. 4-33.
Bias strip.

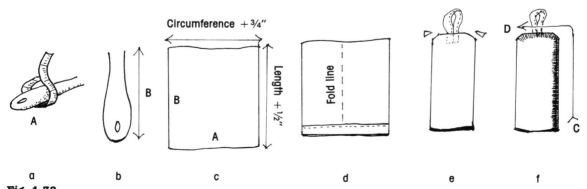

Fig. 4-32.
Another sleeve construction method.

binding to get a sufficient length, lay
the pieces right sides together, at right
angles to each other (Fig. 4-33b), and
sew a ¼″ seam. Press seam open.

If you wish to make bias binding in
longer lengths, there are several work-
able methods. The following seems as
easy as any:

1. Work with a rectangular piece of fabric. By folding opposite corners, estab-
lish a parallelogram, cutting off the
folded corners (Fig. 4-34a).

2. Parallel to the diagonal cuts you
have made, mark whatever width you
want bias strips to be (Fig. 4-34b). Trim
excess fabric.

3. With right sides together, fold fabric
into a tube. This will not be a neat tube
but will be somewhat skewed since the
end of each line must match the opposite end of the line next to it. This is
very important. If you do not make the
shift, you will end up with little circles
rather than with a continuous strip of
bias tape. Pin edges with marked mis-
matched lines and sew a ¼″ seam (Fig.
4-34c).

4. Cut on the marked lines. You should
end up with a long strip of bias.

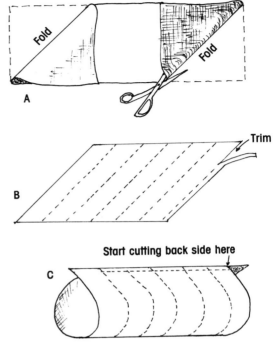

Fig. 4-34.
Continuous bias-binding tape.

All of the instructions that I have
outlined in this chapter are only a
beginning. They are ways that have
worked for me. Please feel free to
change them in any way that will work
better for you.

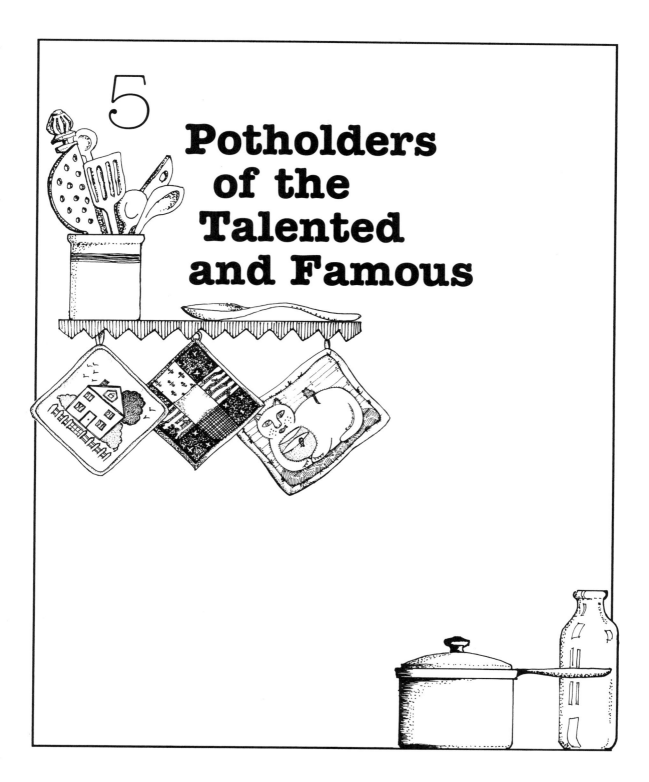

5

Potholders of the Talented and Famous

Artistic Potholders

The potholder's time has come. No longer relegated to the ignominy of life in a kitchen drawer, it has become an item designed and made by artists, displayed as a tiny jewel. Long regarded by fiber artists at the same level that potters regarded ashtrays, potholders now provide a creative challenge not belittled by their size and culinary destination.

Nancy Gano's sculptural potholder is an example of this (Fig. 5-1). A spin-off from Nancy's elegant and large soft sculptures, it is constructed of nonwale corduroy, appliquéd with a precise machine satin stitch, and then stuffed and machine quilted. The colors are rich—royal blue, teal, orange, and turquoise. While perhaps too stiff for actual use, it nonetheless functions, when hung within view, to remind us that there is more to kitchen duty than peeling potatoes.

Paying homage to the Dutch painter Piet Mondrian, Bets Ramsey uses traditional quilters' techniques to present a stark, modern potholder—crisp black and white with minimal touches of primary color. Bets pieces and appliqués and then enriches the severe geometry with tiny, even quilting stitches to produce a serene, sophisticated effect (Fig. 5-2).

In contrast, Joan Schulze's cheerful morning sun seems to burst upon the scene spontaneously, waking us better

Fig. 5-1.
Nancy Gano's potholder is actually a small sculpture. It's 12″ long, including the hanging loop.

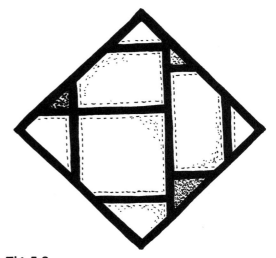

Fig. 5-2.
Who can say that Bets Ramsey's Mondrianesque hot pad is not a work of art? It's 10″ square.

than a second cup of coffee. Working with textile paints, she brushed, splatter-printed, stenciled, and printed the sun's strong face with a rubber stamp she cut from an eraser. The back side of Joan's potholder has a repeat pattern printed from this rubber-eraser stamp. Machine quilting further defines the lively design. (See color section.)

Making good use of a wide variety of decorative stitches on her Bernina 1130, Clydine Peterson appliqués and quilts simultaneously. Starting with filler, she lays on pieces, one after the other, in a crazy patch mode. Clydine folds some pieces over the edge of the filler, continuing on the other side, giving a finished edge to the potholder without the necessity of binding. This method results in a potholder with two equally decorative sides. Sometimes, because of a change in thickness—a seam on the other side, perhaps—the machine might skip a stitch or even several, but Clydine chooses to ignore this, treating the irregular stitching as a sensitive drawing line.

Winder Baker collects all manner of textile items that most of us ignore at garage and estate sales and calls them "daily textiles." Among her daily textiles are, of course, potholders, and her favorites are those made by an aged women, who is now deceased. Though hampered by poor eyesight and perhaps stiff fingers, this woman compulsively made potholders and gave them away. They were fashioned from pieces of a robe (with a corner of pocket showing), a bit of flannel shirting, or a lacy piece of lingerie and were stitched with huge half-inch stitches of coarse yarn. Their stuffing is thick and lumpy. While they

truly are crude, they still imply an energy and spirit that make them memorable. That elderly women never thought of fame or recognition, but the sympathetic yet discerning eye of Winder has saved them for their moment of glory.

Most of us would probably disdain looper potholders as a medium for serious artistic exploration. Arguing this attitude are two looper potholders owned by Phyllis Dukes and woven as part of a series by Lisa Deiches as careful studies of various painters' work.

A work of art in and of itself is the series of machine drawings done by Jane McElroy in a potholder format. Eight separate pieces trace the preparation and presentation of food, from raw materials to a final cup of tea. (Figs. 5-3, 5-4, 5-5, and 5-6). As delicate as fine pen drawings, the food images are surrounded by tiny pin tucks and log cabin patchwork borders. Jane sews on a Bernina 930, and all quilting and drawing were done with a darning foot, lowered feed dogs, and a straight-stitch throat plate. The pin tucks were done with a double needle—providing two colors of thread—and a pin-tucking foot. Amazingly, the back side is quilted in a totally separate design, achieved by Jane's making two separate miniquilts, a front and a back, and joining them only at the bound edges. Designed to be hung side by side in their logical order, these exquisite line drawings would enhance any kitchen or dining area.

Vicki Johnson, a quilt artist living near the California coast, takes the coast, its waters, and its flora and fauna as inspiration for her fabric art.

Fig. 5-3, 5-4, 5-5, 5-6.
Delicate line drawings tell a story of food in Jane McElroy's potholders. Each is 9½″ square.

Textile paint with appliqué, piecing, and quilting done by machine are her techniques. In a marine-inspired potholder, 11″ square, Vicki painted directly on the cotton fabric and added appliquéd seaweed and quilting, both done on her Bernina 1230. She uses Versatex textile paints for most of her color work, changing to Createx for metallic touches. Hanging in a kitchen on a hot summer day, this luminous underwater potholder would, at least, give the cook cool thoughts. (See color section.)

Another artist inspired by the rich visual treasures of the Pacific coast is Pat Shipley, who picked up feathers along the Oregon beaches and laid them on blueprint-sensitive fabric. When exposed to light, the fabric turns a deep indigo. The feathers—or other objects—block out the light in varying degrees; when removed, they leave images of white or paler shades of indigo, according to how much light has crept through. Pat backed and bound her hot pad in blending shades of blue cotton fabric. (See color section.)

Sometimes sheer panic can lead to creativity. The stitchery group with which I am allied sponsors juried fiber arts shows periodically. One unproductive year, I faced the deadline with nothing to enter. I considered revamping a piece I had started some years earlier but had never completed. Since I have always encouraged my students to take risks—if a piece doesn't work, turn it upside down, dye it, or cut it apart and reassemble it—I decided to take my own advice. I cut the incomplete work into pieces and added raw-edged appliqúe shapes with machine

stitching in a showy color, quilting with those same stitched lines. Binding and a hanging loop transformed my three squares into potholders, which I entered as a set. The jury accepted them. (See color section.)

Competitions are great motivators. In yet another year, I learned that the county fair had, for the first time, a category for "The Ultimate Potholder." This tickled my fancy and started my wheels turning. What could translate as "utlimate"? Since I prefer to work with materials that I have at hand rather than shopping for new ones—this dictates boundaries that are easier for me to handle than when I have vast choices—I looked through my treasure trove of fabrics and found metallics. What could be more ultimate? Although this fabric type was perhaps not practical, the fair's entry requirements hadn't mentioned practicality, so I fashioned my potholder from gold-, silver-, and copper-toned metallic fabrics with a black-and-gold brocade to add contrast, along with three dangling crystal beads to give it the final glitz. I called it "Log Cabin Refined" because the design was based on the log cabin quilt square construction. It won a blue ribbon and a silver tray. (See color section.)

Some years ago, ahead of the crowd, Win Ng (1936–1991), a partner in the stylish San Francisco housewares and gift firm of Taylor & Ng, used his whimsical drawing skills to design a series of potholders that were mass-produced and sold by the store. Animals were the dominant subject matter, a hungry cat being my favorite, with a mouse on his back, a fishbowl grasped in his front legs, and his claws bared. Ng's drawings were signed and copyrighted (Fig. 5-7).

It is surprising that of all the contemporary one-of-a-kind potholders I've seen, with many made by prominent fiber artists, very few have been signed. Ordinarily, these artists would not think of leaving their work unsigned. Even though they find a potholder worthy of their creative talents, the potholder remains, as so often in the past, anonymous. If you make unique potholders, you might at least initial them. Date them, too. The few old ones I have found that were dated were enhanced by that date, especially for historians and researchers. I suppose the reason so few sign their potholders is that they expect them to be used and assume that they will not live for other generations to see and wonder.

One potholder that has lived past its allotted time and has risen to greater

heights is a quaint automobile-shaped holder whose wheels are snap-on potholders. Two chubby children occupy the vehicle. The colored design appears to have been printed as a kit, which was further defined by embroidery. Internationally recognized assemblage artist Ray Ward, best known for his athletic compositions, has incorporated this 1920s or 1930s piece into one of his inventive constructions. These potholders never dreamed of riding such a rig. (See color section.)

Favorite Potholders of Celebrity Chefs

If potholders designed by artists carry artistic prestige, wouldn't those favored by celebrity cooks merit recognition at the practical level? I asked several well-known chefs what their favorite kind of potholder is, and the overwhelming choice was a folded towel. Martin Yan, the chef/host of the televised "Yan Can Cook," points out that most professional chefs probably use a towel because they can never find a potholder, yet a towel is always at hand. Yan also says that Chinese home cooks prefer a towel for wok cooking, although he admits to having a few regular potholders near his home oven door.

Alice Waters of Chez Panisse fame, who is credited as the mother of California cuisine featuring garden-fresh ingredients, admits to using in her home kitchen whatever potholders people give her. Her favorites are a flat potholder

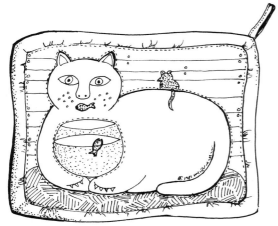

Fig. 5-7.
Win Ng drew a contented cat to grace the potholders sold in his shop in San Francisco.

that is a map of Michigan and a fish-shaped mitt. However, at the restaurant, the towel wins again.

One advantage in using a towel is that it does double duty, serving to cleanse and dry hands as well as acting as a potholder. So towels have come full circle as potholders, from country kitchens of much earlier days to restaurant kitchens of today's haute cuisine.

Even though we may not be famous, we all have talent, perhaps in varying degrees. Sparked by what you've seen and read here, let your mind embrace a sense of play; let it gambol through fields of why-nots and let's-try-its. There is so little to risk in making a potholder—so risk! If the result is not what you aspired to, reupholster it or put it in with the camping equipment, but you just might create a masterpiece to sell at a craft fair, to give as a wedding gift, or to enter in the county fair. The potholder may be your stepping-stone to attaining your fifteen minutes of fame allotted to all of us by the late painter Andy Warhol.

6

Taking Potholders Out of the Kitchen

Clothing and Accessories

What challenge is left in the world of potholders? Everything's been done—or has it? What else can a potholder do or be?

Consider a knockout potholder as the pocket on a garment. You might use one you already have or create one or a matched pair for a specific piece of clothing. A well-known fashion designer placed two old-fashioned looper potholders on a colorful suit jacket several seasons ago, echoing the woven texture in the collar and in the skirt. Patchwork or appliqué potholder pockets in elegant fabrics could change a simple garment into a unique showpiece (Fig. 6-1).

Artist Bonnie Stone does exquisite pen drawings, but she also plays with creative clothing. Using potholder treasures she finds at flea markets and estate sales, she embellishes simple ready-made garments to make them one of a kind. Crocheted apple potholders gleam, perched on the shoulders and as a pocket on Bonnie's black vest. (See color section.) She has also constructed a potholder-plus collage on a high-style blue denim shirt—striking and sure to break the ice at any party, if you don't mind being the center of attention.

Marilyn Green (also known as the "Button Queen") suggests that a child might use a pocket potholder as a snug sleeping bag for a tiny doll (Fig. 6-2). (You can find instructions for making pocket potholders in Chapters 4 and 7.)

Fig. 6-1.
A potholder can make a fashion statement.

You might wish to make the doll too. There are many dollmaking books available.

A colorful potholder made in Thailand by displaced Laotians inspires the next project. Folded in half and stitched up two sides, this bright, ethnic hot pad is transformed instantly into a handsome glasses case. Any square quilted potholder could be treated in the same manner. (See color section.)

If the safety belt of your automobile cuts your neck, just whisk out a softly padded potholder, fold it over the belt,

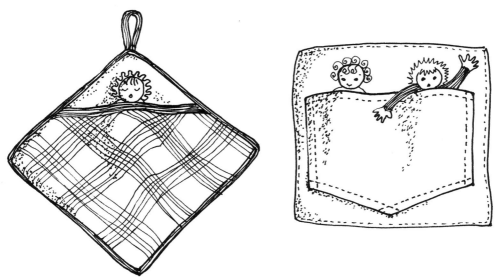

Fig. 6-2.
Pocket potholders can also be used as a snug sleeping bag for a tiny doll.

and stitch up one side, forming a sliding sleeve that, when paced at the proper spot, will lessen the friction against your irritated skin. Better yet, secure it with a Velcro fastening so it can be removed for laundering.

For a needle case, fold a lightly padded 5½″ potholder in half and give it a button or a tie fastening. The filler should be very thin and flexible, such as thin quilt batting or one layer of soft flannel. In the needle case, a piece of wool fabric can be stitched inside to hold the needles. Extra "pages" of wool could be sewn in to hold more needles or a pocket could be incorporated to hold small scissors (Figs. 6-3; color section).

Fold a large soft potholder and tie it for use as a wrapping (Fig. 6-4). Simple

Fig. 6-3.
A small potholder is folded in half and given a button fastening to form a needle case.

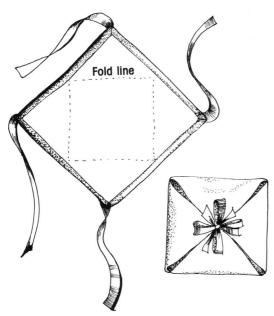

Fig. 6-4.
A large ribboned hot pad becomes a tied wrapping for a small gift.

Fig. 6-5.
A table runner made by several friends should be planned carefully to please the recipient.

origami techniques suggest other soft wrapping forms.

Potholders That Work Together

Several hot pads sewn together in a preplanned arrangement give focus to a dining table as a runner (Fig. 6-5). This may serve as decoration only or may also protect the table surface from hot serving dishes. This might be considered as a form of lap quilting, sewing and quilting the modules before slip-stitching them together. Of course, the advantage of this type of construction is that the small units are easy to slip into your purse or pocket so that you can work on them while waiting in the den-

tist's office or while watching the game at the soccer field. It would also work well as a group project, with each person working with similar colors and a chosen theme or pattern.

Another item that a group could assemble is a fabric container—a box or a wrapping. Six small, stiffly stuffed potholders could be whipped together to form a soft receptacle for precious treasures (Fig. 6-6). Five potholders with

Fig. 6-6.
Try assembling stiffly stuffed potholder units made by several individuals for a group-constructed gift box.

minimal stuffing would make a wrapping for a flat object, such as a handmade book or a special keepsake photograph. The outside might be plain fabric in a rich texture, such as velvet, while the inside surfaces, revealed when the wrapping is untied, could be surprise miniature stitcheries characteristic of the individual makers (Fig. 6-7).

A space divider or screen is an ambitious project, but Nancy Gano assembled sixty-four colorful potholders to answer that challenge. (See color section.) Using nonwale corduroy in brilliant colors, she appliquéd shapes with a machine satin stitch to form the potholders. As Nancy appliquéd, she in-

serted a ribbon on each of the four sides of the potholders for ease in the final assembly. You might try arranging square potholders on point for another effect (Fig. 6-8). Again, this could be a group or a family project.

Some years ago, Bets Ramsey started a progressive quilted wall hanging depicting special events and places in the lives of her family members. Starting at the center with the image of their present family home, Bets added individual units, each one constructed like a potholder. Silhouettes of states where they have lived, musical instruments the children have played, titles of books written by her poet husband,

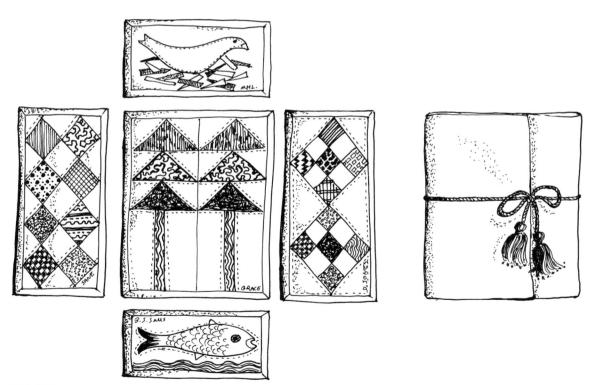

Fig. 6-7.
The decorative surfaces may be turned to the inside on this soft wrapping.

Fig. 6-8.
Potholders used as a space divider will also absorb sound.

symbols of unusual happenings—all these are pictured on different-size potholder units and then fitted and stitched into the ever-changing wall hanging. An unexpected bonus of Bets's construction method is the varigated back side, the separate units having different back fabrics. You might try this idea as a family project, with each family member contributing a square. Of course, you should have a master plan so that odd-sized blocks will fit (Fig. 6-9).

The same method could be used for a small doll quilt. The first consideration is scale; shrink decorative elements proportionate to the small size of the doll quilt. Three potholder units are required—one for the top and two for the drop at the sides. A quilt made in this way and seamed with a slip stitch will "break" at the edge of the mattress and hang more like a full-scale quilt than one made as a whole top (Fig. 6-10).

While we're thinking about miniatures, a five minute or less project for a dollhouse kitchen is a potholder, of course. Just zigzag around a 1⅛″ square of prequilted fabric, add a yarn loop, and there you have it.

A minimum of twelve cotton looper potholders sewn together make a sturdy bath mat (Fig. 6-11). Weave the loopers in colors and patterns that complement your bathroom, and play with their arrangement before sewing or crocheting them together. I heard of a bedspread made in this manner, but sheer weight would seem to rule this out as a practical possibility.

To introduce her sons to weaving, Clydine Peterson showed them how to thread a small, square looper-type loom with yarn left over from her own weaving. Son Robert, who has gone on to more serious construction, such as making his own hover-type craft from scratch, showed his inventiveness even at age four by producing a droll little doll from his woven potholders (Fig. 6-12). This is an idea that could be further explored.

Just suppose that one day you should produce a potholder that is like a miniature abstract painting. Mount in on a blending piece of fabric and tuck it into a Plexiglas frame. You have created your own tiny masterpiece, perhaps worthy of a place in the parlor.

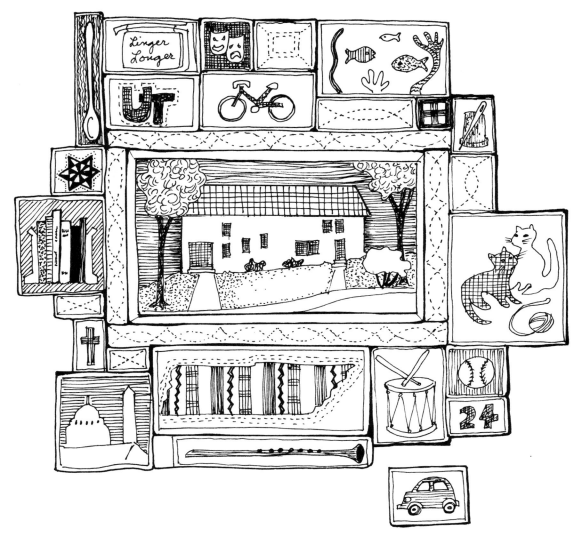

Fig. 6-9.
A family quilt grows as potholderlike units are added.

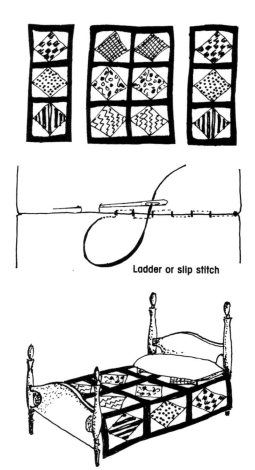

Ladder or slip stitch

Fig. 6-10.
A doll quilt constructed of three potholder units hangs plumb at the sides.

Fig. 6-11.
Making a cotton looper bath mat should keep a preteen busy for several days during a summer vacation.

Fig. 6-12.
Robert Peterson made this lanky potholder doll when he was only four. Collection Clydine Peterson.

The potential for creativity in individual potholders, and in more involved projects employing potholders or potholder techniques, is an inviting open door. Let your imagination run free through that door and into the boundless creative spaces beyond. Only your imagination defines the limits.

Hot Potholder Projects

In chapter 4, I provided general instructions about constructing potholders and urged you to create your own designs and to improvise construction methods. I hope you will do that as it's much more fun and relaxing than following exacting directions. I hope you'll pick up odd scraps and compose them into your own unique creations. Don't feel restricted by rules; there are none, so make up your own! Try oddball ideas that you might not want to risk on a pillow for the living room or a quilt. You don't need to invest in expensive materials. Except for experimental filler, I made all the potholders for this book from materials I already had at home. You don't have to be an accomplished needleworker and you certainly don't need sophisticated equipment. You just have to be willing to take a few small risks.

However, if you feel a little doubtful about diving hip deep into improvisation, you will find step-by-step instructions for making a range of potholders in this chapter. (See color section.) Please feel free to change them in any way and to make improvements in the construction methods.

First, a word or two about the instructions which follow:

- When batting is called for, cotton is preferable.
- Usually, when a particular filler is called for, others may be substituted.
- Binding does not always have to be bias; straight-grain binding is often acceptable.
- When bias binding is required, use commercial 1″ binding or cut your own 1½″ wide.

If you are making only one potholder requiring a particular color of bias binding, cut just enough for the potholder and loop. Lay a straight edge at a 45° angle to the selvage of your fabric and cut the needed length with a rotary cutter. Measure 1½″ width and cut again. If you do not have a rotary cutter, mark your fabric and cut with scissors. If you need longer lengths of bias binding, see the instructions near the end of chapter 4.

I have given a list of materials needed for each project. If you have a scrap bag of resources, you will usually not need as much yardage as called for, and of course, the leftovers from one potholder are the beginnings of another. So read through the instructions for a project to get a more accurate idea of what you need to buy as opposed to what you have.

Bird's Nest

This project will incorporate machine appliqué and will be constructed by the pillow-slip method discussed in chapter 4.

1. You will need ¼ yard "nest colored" fabric (yellow or tan) and some tiny scraps of blending colors for nesting material (step 9), scraps of toweling for filler, scraps of egg color (I used soft blue), paper-backed fusible web, four inches of bias tape (or make your own), and sewing thread in appropriate colors.

2. Cut oval nest shape for front and back of potholder, adding ½" seam allowance to the pattern given. Back may be a different fabric from front (Fig. 7-1B).

3. Cut two layers toweling in oval nest shape without adding seam allowance.

4. Pin front fabric to both layers toweling.

5. Following instructions on the package, bond paper-backed fusible web to fabric you have chosen for the eggs. Three close shades of the same color will be more interesting than three eggs of the same fabric. You will need to bond only a small piece of each fabric.

6. Cut eggs exact size, no seam allowance (Fig. 7-1B).

7. Bond eggs to nest shape, placing them as shown in the drawing.

8. Machine appliqué with satin stitch in a color closely related to that of the eggs.

9. Cut nesting material from four or more fabrics. These do not need to be bonded. Elongated triangles and trapezoidal bars work well as nesting material.

10. Lay these on the lower half of the nest, letting them overlap the eggs slightly. Pin some on and appliqué with a straight stitch, sewing rather randomly to suggest more nesting material. Adding more shapes, try to secure the small pieces so that will stay where you put them. The edges will be fringed and frayed, but this lends to the nest effect. Straight stitches continued above the eggs will finish the decorative part of your potholder.

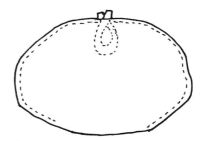

Fig. 7-1A.
The loop is pinned inside, as shown, before stitching the seam.

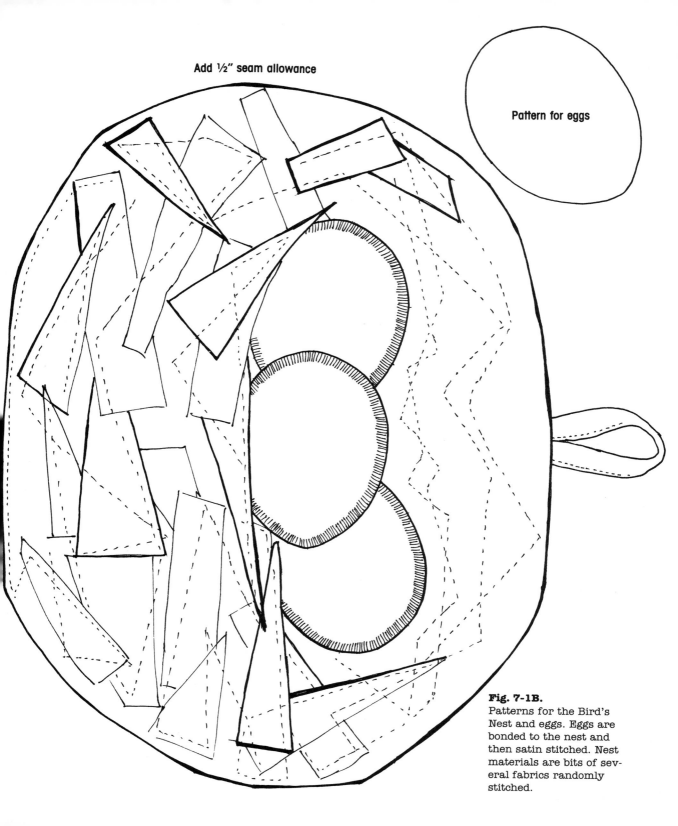

Add ½" seam allowance

Pattern for eggs

Fig. 7-1B.
Patterns for the Bird's
Nest and eggs. Eggs are
bonded to the nest and
then satin stitched. Nest
materials are bits of several fabrics randomly
stitched.

11. Stitch a 4″ length of bias tape for hanging loop or make your own from fabric, either bias or straight grain.

12. Placing back and front right sides together, pin loop between them (Fig. 7-1A).

13. Stitch just outside the edge of filler, leaving an opening at bottom.

14. Turn right side out. Pin edges of lower opening to inside and stitch.

Free Chevron

This potholder is worked in a stitch-and-press technique and is finished by the mitered corner method. The design looks good in analogous colors plus an accent color. I have worked it in shades of purple, plum, lavender, and, for a little spice, burnt orange and rust. Try blues shading to aquas accented with chartreuse or try reds and red-oranges that need no accent other than themselves. You might top a Christmas package of a new cookbook with a potholder of different greens along with a spot of holly berry red.

1. You will need an 8″ square of medium-weight firm fabric, a square of batting slightly larger, a 10″ square of fabric for backing, several colors (bits of each) for the chevron, and sewing thread.

2. Cut an 8″ square of firm fabric, such as denim or lightweight canvas. This will not show in the finished potholder.

3. Lay a layer of thin batting over this. It can be slightly larger than the fabric square. Baste together.

4. Fig. 7-2 shows order in which pieces are sewn.

5. Lay a triangle of fabric (piece 1) right side up along one edge (Fig. 7-3a). Pin in place.

6. Cut a strip of fabric (piece 2) 1½″ wide and 3½″ long and lay right side down on top of the triangle (Fig. 7-3b).

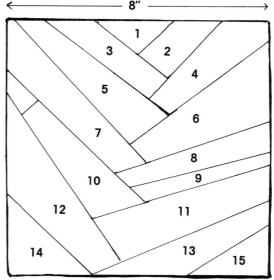

Fig. 7-2.
Diagram for the free chevron. Pieces are sewn over a layer of fabric and batting in the order shown in the stitch-and-press technique.

7. Seam and flip piece 2 back (Fig. 7-3b) to show right side. At this point, pin piece 2 so that it lies flat (Fig. 7-3c). Although the name of this process, stitch and press, implies pressing with an iron, doing so would flatten the work excessively. Just press it with your fingers and pin.

8. Cut piece 3. From here on, you make the choices of width and shape. The strips may be wider at one end than the other and the effect is more interesting if they do vary.

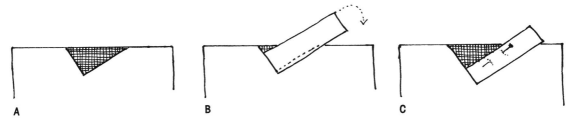

Fig. 7-3.
(A) Lay triangle. (B) Sew, then flip. (C) Pin strip 2 flat.

9. Proceed from side to side until square is filled. Notice that in Fig. 7-2, pieces 8 and 9 were sewn side by side before swinging to the other side for piece 10. This is an arbitrary design choice following the precept that the unexpected makes a visual image more interesting. Piece 10 is made of two pieces, a similar decision.

10. Trim edges of pieces and of batting to same size as foundation square (Fig. 7-4).

11. Cut backing fabric 10″ square. Lay pieced square in center of the wrong side of it. Pin in place (Fig. 7-5a).

12. Stitch in the ditch through several seams to secure the layers in position.

13. Fold potholder diagonally, right side up. Stitch backing for about ⅜″ at corners of front piece and at right angles to fold. Backstitch to secure. Trim corners (Fig. 7-5b).

14. Turn backing to front, turning under edges. Pin and topstitch. (Review chapter 4 for more detailed instruction.)

15. Form a loop of bias or straight-cut fabric and stitch to back at corner or see my serendipitous solution.

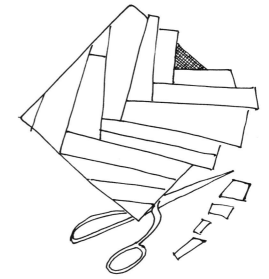

Fig. 7-4.
Trim edges.

As I finished my free chevron hot pad and before making the loop, I spied a torn strip of the backing fabric approximately ½″ wide. It was soft fabric. I stuck it under the pressor foot and zigzagged over it twice lengthwise to fashion a nice satiny cord for my loop. The bobbin thread is orange while the top thread is plum colored; the effect is stunning (Fig. 7-6).

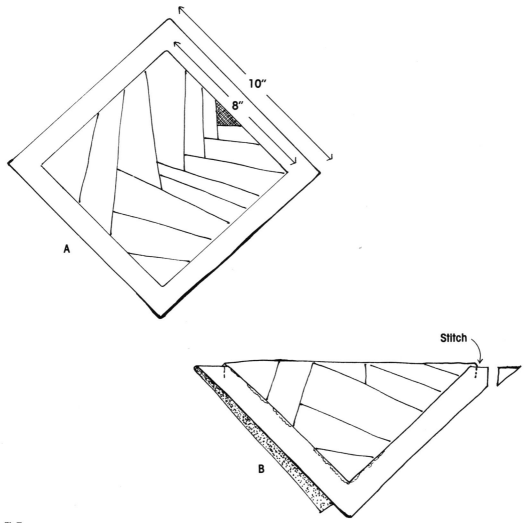

Fig. 7-5.
Lay the 8″ chevron square on wrong side of the 10″ backing. Quilt. Fold diagonally, right side up, stitch, and trim.

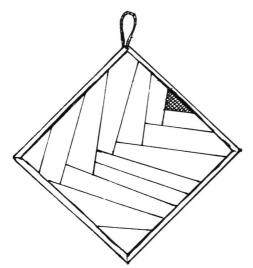

When finished, I realized that one of the fabrics in the chevron showed crease lines from some previous life. As this looked rather shabby, I set my trusty zigzag stitch again and covered the lines. I often use this method to cover a mistake or to give an accent.

These two spontaneous actions show the kind of attitude I'm hoping to instill in you. Experiment! There's no telling what you'll discover.

Fig. 7-6.
Finish the chevron potholder with an improvised loop.

Fancy Trim Easter Egg

The colorful trims belie the quick construction of this piece which follows the Free and Easy method in chapter 4.

1. You will need bits of various trims, sewing thread, a 6″ by 7″ piece each of fabric for the front, prequilted fabric for the back, and toweling for filler.

2. Cut top fabric (nonquilted), backing of prequilted fabric, and one layer of toweling exact size pattern (Fig. 7-7). No seam allowance on any of these.

3. Sandwich the toweling between the other two fabrics with their right sides out. Pin a loop of braid or rickrack at the top, tucking its ends within the sandwich. Pin all layers together.

4. Arrange strips of rickrack, braid, and trims in a distribution pleasing to you. Stitch them through layers with a straight stitch.

5. Trim edges.

6. Stay stitch the edge of the egg. Then lay a cord (number 8 pearl cotton) along the edge and zigzag over it with an open stitch, and then again with a satin stitch. An alternative for making an edge that does not ripple is water-soluble stabilizer. There are several brands on the market. Laid under or over the edge to be stitched, the stabilizer may be torn away after zig-zagging, and any remaining may be washed away with cold water.

Fig. 7-7.
Pattern for Easter egg with fancy trims. Choose bright or pastel trims that you have on hand.

Christmas Potholder

This one is done by Janie Warnick's speedy, easy method outlined in chapter 4. I use a prequilted fabric that is bright red on one side and a red-and-white check on the other. The cookie cutter Christmas tree is kelly green with white polka dots. I used rickrack for the loop because its wobbly line echoes the wobbly line of the tree (Fig. 7-8).

1. You will need enough prequilted fabric to cut two 6″ circles, a bit of fabric for the tree and paper-backed fusible web the same size, sewing thread, and rickrack for the loop.

2. Using a saucer (6″ in diameter) as your pattern, cut two pieces of prequilted fabric. If you're comfortable with your rotary cutter and its blade is sharp, cut directly against the saucer. If not, mark around the dish and cut with your scissors.

3. Cut a 4″ length of rickrack.

4. Turn your quilted fabric so that quilting lines go in the same direction on both pieces. This looks neater.

5. Decide if you want both sides to be the same color or if each side should show a different side of the quilted fabric. I did the latter.

6. Slash the center of the side on which you intend to place your appliqué.

7. With circles turned wrong side out, place rickrack loop between the two circles with rickrack ends matching the raw edges of the circle fabric.

8. Stitch all the way around in a generous ⅛″ seam. Turn.

9. Run a sharp instrument all along the seam to give a sharp edge. Press.

10. With a straight stitch, top stitch ⅛″ to ¼″ from the edge of the circle.

11. Bond the paper-backed fusible web to the back of Christmas tree fabric. Trace around the pattern in Fig. 7-8 or use your own Christmas tree cookie cutter, marking the paper side.

12. Following the paper-backed fusible web instructions, bond the appliqué over the slash and follow with a satin stitch around the edge of the tree.

Fig. 7-8.
This Christmas tree was traced from a cookie cutter. Trace it or make your own pattern.

Carrots the Free and Easy Way

Here's another potholder done in the Free and Easy method of construction. However, the decorative work will take some time.

Choose two shades of orange for the carrots and a green print for the tops. The back may be of a compatible print. You will also need batting and toweling for filler, and orange and green sewing thread.

1. Cut backing fabric and one of the orange fabrics the exact size of the entire pattern, no seam allowance (Fig. 7-9a).

2. Cut one layer toweling and one layer batting sightly smaller than above pieces.

3. Cut single carrot from second orange fabric and tops from the green print. To create patterns for these, trace around Fig. 7-9a using contour drawings B and C as your guides.

4. Stack with backing, right side down, on the bottom. Toweling next with batting on top of that and large orange piece on top with its right side up. Pin the single carrot and the tops securely in place.

5. Stay-stitch the outer edge.

6. Stitch outer edge with zigzag stitch over a cord, using thread of slightly darker orange around the carrots. Wait to zigzag the tops.

7. With the orange thread, appliqué the single carrot with three rows of straight stitch. These do not need to be precisely spaced but may move easily along the edge of the carrot, leaving the edge raw. After all, carrots are kind of hairy before peeling.

8. Outline the shape and contours of the carrots with straight stitch. You may want to mark these lightly before you stitch if you don't feel secure drawing freehand with a sewing-machine needle.

9. Changing to green thread, zigzag the outer edge of the carrot tops over a cord.

10. Quilt the carrot tops with free-machine embroidery in a free, loopy line. This requires a bit of practice on a scrap potholder. An embroidery hoop is not necessary because the potholder is very firm at this point. On my Elna, I used a darning spring rather than the usual foot.

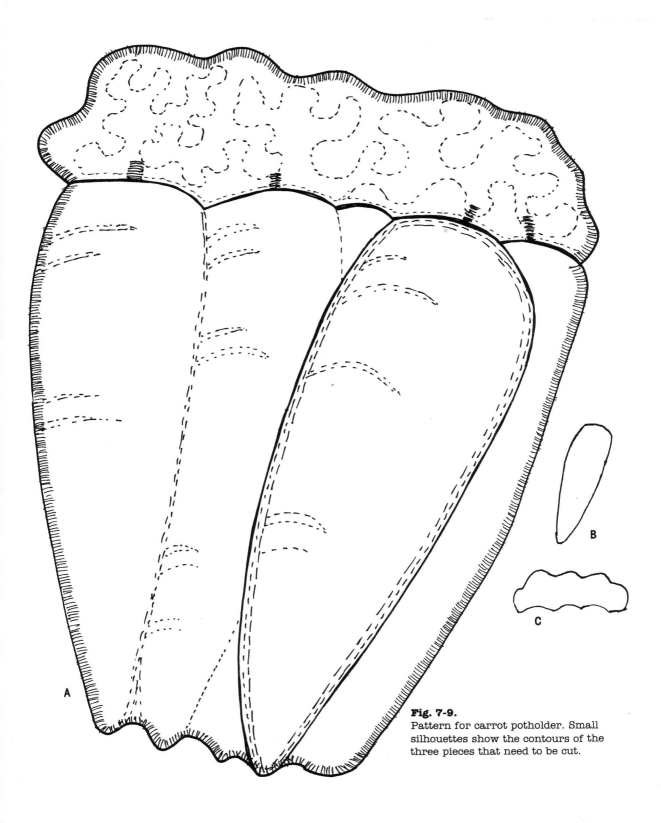

Fig. 7-9.
Pattern for carrot potholder. Small
silhouettes show the contours of the
three pieces that need to be cut.

Slipcover Potholder

This is a quick potholder to make, especially if you have a clever print fabric for the front so that you don't have to do any decorative work. I made it up with a graphic print of two farm girls clasping a basket between them, their size dictating the dimensions of the hot pad—6¾". I used toweling and batting as filler and denim as the back fabric. I loved the result and had planned to use a magnet as the hanging device but found that the weight of the piece required four of the "craft" magnets I purchased at the hardware store, making it even heavier.

Lighter weight fabrics and filler and a 6" square would help to diminish the number of magnets to two, so that is the plan I will outline below.

1. You will need a 6½" square of fabric for the front, ¼ yard lightweight fabric, 6" square of table felt, magnet(s), and sewing thread.

2. Cut one 6" square table felt. Zigzag its edges.

3. Cut a rectangle of thin cotton 2" by 1½" and stitch it to the table felt to make a tiny upside-down pocket (Fig. 7-10a). (This will enable you to try different numbers of magnets later before you sew up the pocket.)

4. Cut decorative fabric 6½" square.

5. Cut two pieces lightweight fabric measuring 6½" by 4½" for back.

6. Put a tiny hem along one long side of each of the back pieces.

7. Place decorative fabric and back pieces with right sides together, matching raw edges. The two hemmed edges will overlap near the center (Fig. 7-10b).

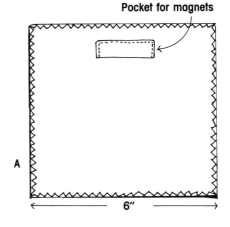

Pocket for magnets

A

6"

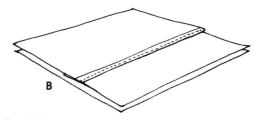

B

Fig. 7-10.
The magnet pocket is sewn to the zigzagged table felt on three sides only (a). Two back pieces will overlap when sewn to the front piece of the slipcover (b).

8. Stitch around outer edge and trim corners.

9. Turn right side out and insert table felt.

10. Place magnets in pocket and try the hot pad on the refrigerator. If it holds, remove table felt and stitch fourth side of magnet pocket. If not, try adding another magnet or add a hanging loop to the slipcover.

Spiral Sun

Colleen Williams's spiral star shown in chapter 4 is the direct inspiration for this hot pad. The principal decorative effect stems from free-machine quilting (Fig. 7-11). If you are not practiced in this skill, try a rehearsal run on something that doesn't matter. Not heeding my own advice, I plunged right in and ended up with a shaky sun. This doesn't bother me, though, because it evokes images of the throbbing heat that emanates from the sun, but if you are a perfectionist—practice. To set up your machine for free-machine embroidery, follow instructions in your manual for darning. **Note:** You will need to enlarge the pattern in Fig. 7-11 on a copy machine at 115% to get a potholder 6½" square.

1. You will need ¼ yard of two different colors of fabric, cotton batting, one yard of 1" bias binding, and sewing thread in an appropriate color.

2. Cut 6½" squares of front fabric and two layers of thin cotton batting.

3. Cut backing fabric 7" square to allow for distortion during quilting.

4. Lay backing right side down with batting and front on top of it. Baste so that when you start your spiral of quilting you will not have to avoid or remove pins.

5. Machine quilt with contrasting color thread. Refer to your own sewing machine manual, and for expert advice, see *The Complete Book of Machine Quilting* by Robbie and Tony Fanning (see the Appendix).

6. Trim all edges even.

7. Refer to chapter 4's section on making potholders by the bias-binding method to finish the spiral sun potholder.

Fig. 7-11.
Pattern for spiral sun. Yellow fabric with red or orange stitching will suggest warmth.

Felt Asparagus Potholder

The best and simplest felt pot-holders will be made by children if they are allowed to design their own and to sew them by hand or machine. If you lack the assurance of a child in your designing capabilities, though, try this asparagus potholder. Since felt's washing qualities are dubious, this potholder is appropriate for short-term use or for show only. Construction is quick.

1. You will need two 7″ squares olive green felt, one 7″ square yellow-green felt, ½ yard of red yarn, cord or tape, and sewing thread.

2. Cut two of the overall squarish shape in olive green felt (Fig. 7-12).

3. Cut one piece of lighter yellow/green felt for asparagus shape (see Fig. 7-12 contour guide).

4. Cut yarn 4″ long for hanging loop.

5. Pin all layers together with asparagus shape on top. Tuck yarn loop in place between two dark green layers.

6. Machine stitch around asparagus shapes and use machine stitching to define asparagus heads and shading.

7. Stitch around outer edge of dark green shape, securing yarn loop as you sew.

8. Cut a piece of red yarn, cord, or tape 16″ long. Tie loosely around potholder at the middle and secure in place with hand or machine stitching.

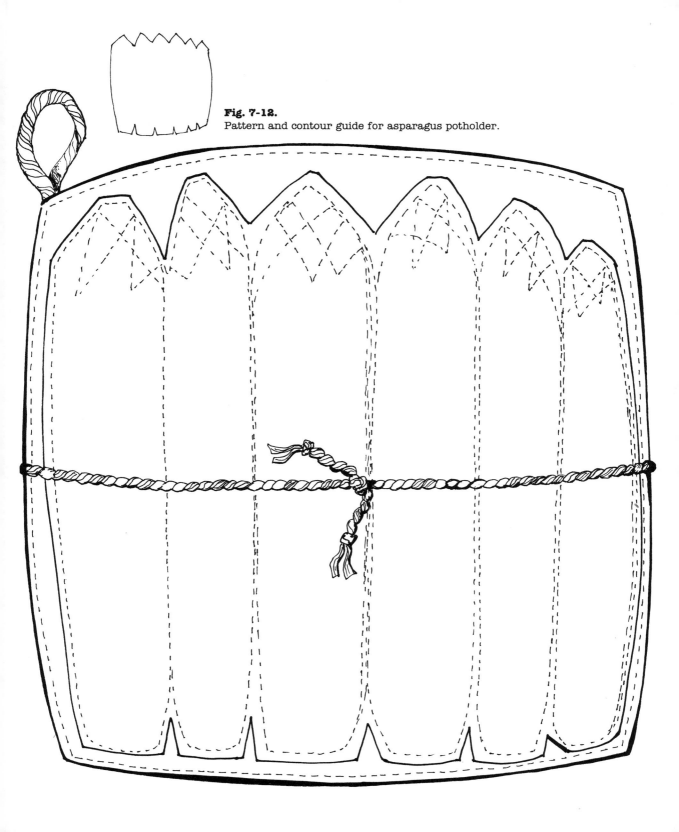

Fig. 7-12.
Pattern and contour guide for asparagus potholder.

Cooking in White Gloves

Surely white gloves will suggest as immaculate an image as anyone wants to project. Double mitt construction is used to give the effect shown in Fig. 7-13.

1. You will need enough prequilted fabric to cut a piece measuring 28″ by 6½″, ¼ yard unquilted fabric for pockets, ¼ yard white fabric such as canvas or duck, ¼ yard paper backed fusible web,

2 yards single fold narrow bias binding, and sewing thread.

2. Cut large pattern piece of prequilted fabric. Be sure to lay the pattern on the fold of the fabric, as shown in the diagram (Fig. 7-14a). The quilted fabric I used seemed too thin, so I doubled it, stitching around the edges for ease of handling during the rest of the sewing process.

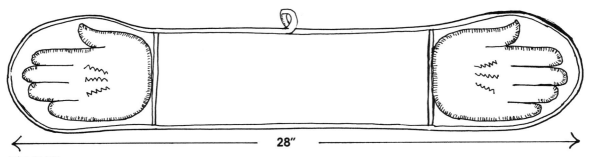

Fig. 7-13.
White gloves dress up a double mitt.

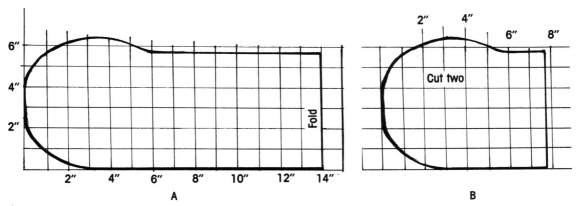

Fig. 7-14.
Pattern for double mitt. Be sure to lay larger piece on the fold, as shown. Each square equals 1″.

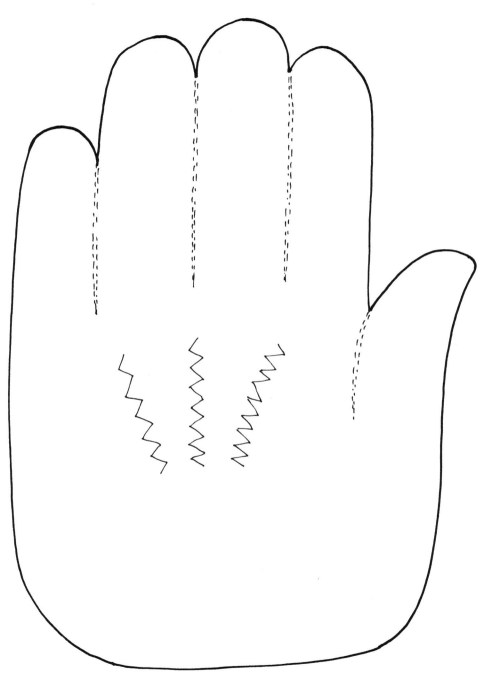

Fig. 7-15.
Pattern for glove appliqué shape and its stitching.

3. Cut two pockets of unquilted fabric (Fig. 7-14b).

4. Bond fabric you have chosen for glove appliqués to paper-backed fusible web according to instructions on the package. If you are making white gloves, be sure the white fabric is opaque enough that the pocket color doesn't show through.

5. Cut glove shapes and bond them to pockets (Fig. 7-15).

6. Zigzag around glove shape with satin stitch.

7. Machine embroider lines on gloves in thread color to match pocket. I used red.

8. Bind straight pocket with single-fold, narrow bias binding. In all, you will need about 90" of bias tape.

9. Refering back to Fig. 7-13, stitch pockets to large quilted shape.

10. Starting at top center, pin right side of bias binding to top (glove) side of mitt around entire mitt and sew as shown in chapter 4's section on making potholders by the bias-binding method, making a loop at the ending point.

Blue Jeans Ride Again

You must know by now that I like blue jeans denim. Here is yet another way to use it, employing Janie Warnick's quick method from chapter 4.

1. You will need an old pair of blue jeans from which you can cut a back pocket, ¼ yard prequilted fabric, 4″ by 6″ piece of paper-backed fusible web, sewing thread, and tape for a loop.

2. Cut a 7″ square from the jeans with the pocket in the center. If your pocket is too large to fit within this measurement, just be sure to allow ¾″ beyond the pocket edges.

3. Cut a square of prequilted fabric the same size as above square. You may notice a line of satin stitching on this fabric in the color photo. This is where I had to piece the prequilted fabric, since I was working with scraps.

4. Cut a slash in the center of prequilted fabric.

5. With right sides together, pin denim and quilted material. Pin 4″ bias tape to inside for loop.

6. Sew all the way around the square. Turn right side out.

7. With sharp instrument, push out corners and seams and press.

8. Bond a 4″ by 6″ piece of paper-backed fusible web to a piece of denim. Trace cowboy boot shape in Fig. 7-16 onto denim and decorate with stitching if you desire.

9. Cut out the boot and iron over the slit according to instructions packet. Do not stitch the edges of the boot at this time as this would stitch through the pocket.

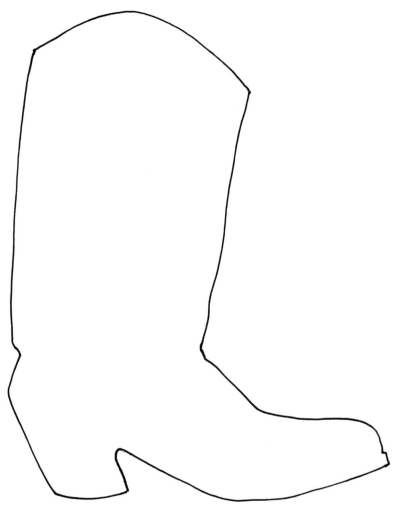

Fig. 7-16.
Cut the cowboy boot from fabric bonded to paper-backed fusible web for the slit closure in the blue jeans potholder.

Alternative: Completely Jeans Potholder

Try making a denim potholder using old jeans fabric throughout—for pocket front, filler, and the backing. All you will need is an old pair of jeans, sewing thread, and cord for a neat edge.

1. Cut hip pocket from jeans with enough surrounding fabric to make 7" square.

2. Cut backing same size.

3. Cut the filler (one or two layers denim) 6¾" square.

4. Stitch filler to wrong side of back fabric in an "X" from corner to corner.

5. Lay backing down with filler side up. Lay pocket piece on top, pocket side up, and zigzag over cord around the edges.

You could make the same denim hot potholder without the pocket. Instead, appliqué the jeans label or use shapes of darker or lighter blue denim on a denim front. Both versions of the completely denim potholder are quick, economical, ecologically sound because of the recycled material, functional, and attractive. In addition, both of the denim pocket potholders work as hot-pot holders or, if the pocket is large enough, as mitts. Or, as mentioned earlier, as sleeping spots for tiny dolls.

Heritage Chicken

I did not consider including a chicken potholder in this book until I realized that chicken potholders are a part of our American heritage. Winterthur Museum owns a Pennsylvania chicken potholder dated between 1800 and 1875 (Fig. 7-17). Constructed of sturdy linen, its wings are dyed red, green, and purple and are outlined with a buttonhole stitch. It sports a red wool comb and wattles and gazes at us with embroidered blue eyes, a truly elegant fowl.

I have found chicken potholders in various pattern books through the years, and have tried several ways of making them. Though not a simple project for a beginner, the one presented here seems to be the easiest (Fig. 7-18). If you want a simpler project, eliminate the appliqué wings. The final finishing is done by the Bias Binding method.

1. You will need ¼ yard of prequilted fabric, a bit of fabric for the wings, red

Fig. 7-17.
This chicken potholder was made between 1800 and 1875. Courtesy, Winterthur Museum.

Fig. 7-18.
Your potholder should look like this.

felt, Ultrasuede, wool or cotton fabric for the comb, one yard of bias binding, small wad of batting, buttons or snaps for the eyes, and sewing thread.

2. From prequilted fabric, cut two each of piece #1 (Fig. 7-19A) and piece #2 (Fig. 7-19B). Mark points X and Y. Be sure to add ¼″ seam allowances. Eyes can be sewn now or on as a final step.

3. Cut two wings from harmonizing fabric. I used a solid yellow.

4. From red fabric, cut comb. Felt, wool, Ultrasuede, or cotton fabric is acceptable.

5. Right sides together, comb pinned to inside, sew the chicken shapes (piece 1) together, stitching from X to Y up over head and back (Fig. 7-20a).

6. Turn right side out and appliqué wing shapes in place, holding the chicken open.

7. Stuff head with batting until it looks and feels right.

8. Sew seam along straight side of piece 2 pieces, right sides together (Fig. 7-20b).

9. Open chicken and pin piece 2 in place with right sides out (Fig. 7-20c). Baste. If edges are rough, trim to match.

10. Cut 28″ of commerical 1″ bias tape. If you are making your own bias, cut it 1½″ wide.

11. Starting ¾″ from the apex of the tail (Y in Fig. 7-20d), pin tape to the edge of the top so that you will sew up over the tail and around the edge of the circle. Right side of tape should be pinned to right side of top. Stitch all the way around to meet the starting point. Do not cut off excess length of tape.

12. Bring tape over the raw edge to the inside and stitch by machine or by hand.

13. Stitch the excess tail end along its edge and then stitch it in place to form a loop.

14. Stitch on buttons or snaps for eyes if you have not already done so.

15. Congratulations! You've just become a part of American history.

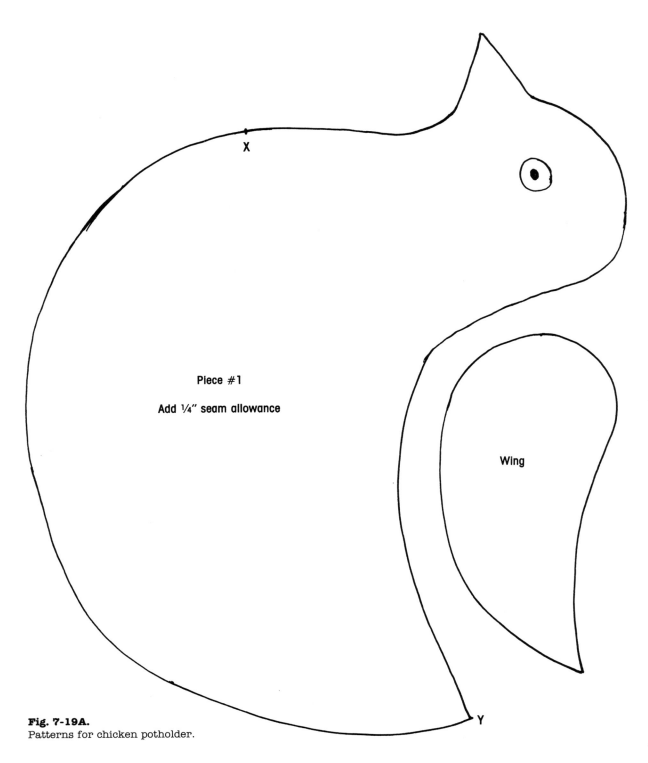

X

Piece #1

Add ¼" seam allowance

Wing

Y

Fig. 7-19A.
Patterns for chicken potholder.

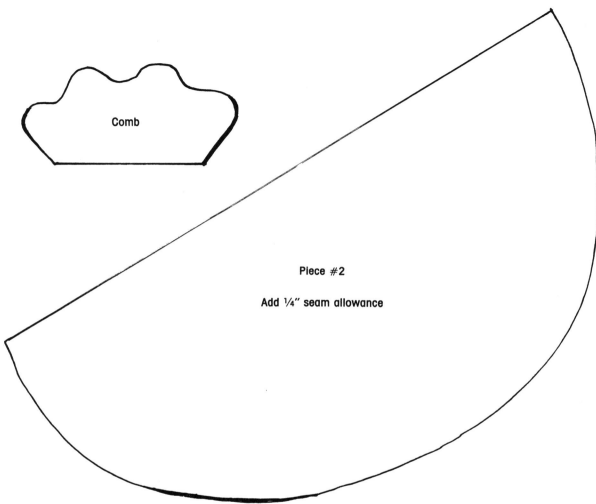

Comb

Piece #2

Add ¼″ seam allowance

Fig. 7-19B.
Patterns for chicken potholder.

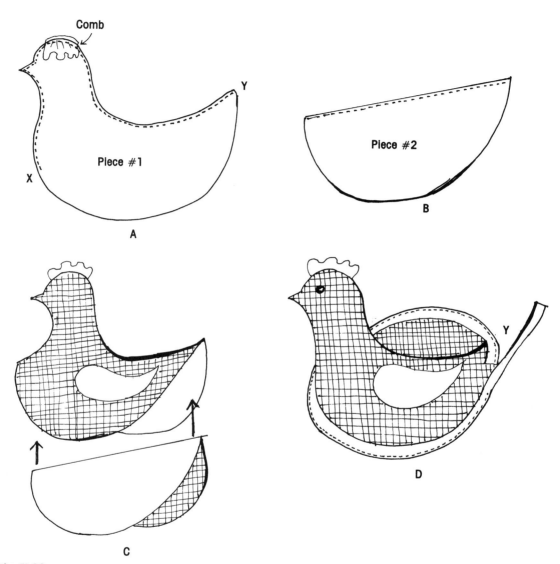

Fig. 7-20.
Assembly of chicken potholder.

Softball Potholder—It's a Hit

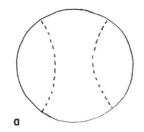
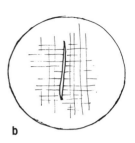

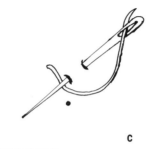
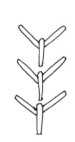

Fig. 7-21A.
Softball potholder stitching diagrams.

If you know someone who would rather play softball than cook, perhaps this potholder will soothe the kitchen crisis. I chose an off-white canvas for the skin of the ball. If you have a decorative stitch on your machine that will duplicate the stitching on the ball and is in the right scale, by all means, use it. Mine was too small for the size of the ball, so I hand embroidered the decorative stitching. Construction is by Janie Warnick's method.

1. You will need ¼ yard white canvas, table felt, red embroidery floss, fabric and paper-backed fusible web to cover slit, and sewing thread.

2. Cut two circles 5½" in diameter. If tracing the pattern shown here, be sure to add seam allowance (Fig 7-21B).

3. On one circle, mark two arcs, see Fig. 7-21A(a). I used a number 2 pencil and drew a dotted line lightly.

4. Cut one circle of table felt 5" in diameter. Pin to back side of marked circle.

5. At this point, following the dotted lines, embroider the softball's seams with red thread. I used a full six-strand embroidery floss to make "Y" stitches, which look true to softball reality. See Fig. 7-21A(c) for "Y" stitch instructions. Stitch all the way through the table felt. Notice that the two lines of stitches go in opposite directions.

6. Cut a 4" by 1¼" piece of canvas and stitch lengthwise with edges turned inside. This will be the loop.

7. Slash the canvas circle that is not embroidered. Refer to Janie Warnick's method in chapter 4 if in doubt. Make the slash on the straight grain as shown in Fig. 7-21A(b).

8. With right sides together and loop pinned inside, sew around entire circle, making a ¼" seam.

9. Turn right side out, push sharp instrument around entire seam, and iron a shape over the slit. (You could use iron-on mending tape.) Again, refer to Janie's method in chapter 4.

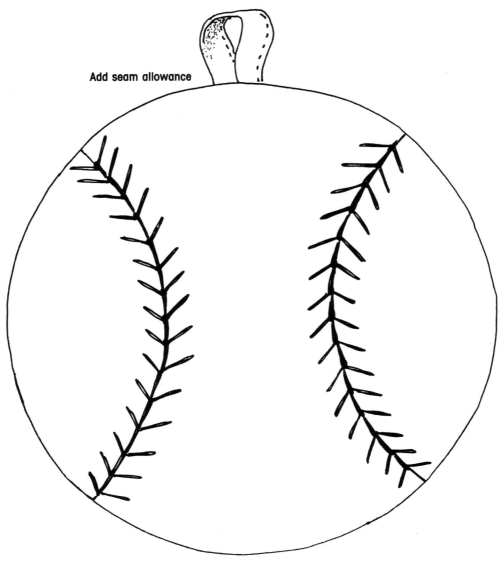

Add seam allowance

Fig. 7-21B.
Softball potholder pattern.

Teddy Bear Potholder

This potholder was adapted from a tiny 4″ felt teddy bear given to my youngest daughter many years ago. It is effective if cut with pinking shears. I sewed mine by hand because I had time at that moment and could not get to my sewing machine. For speed, use your machine. Easy construction. Facial embroidery takes a few extra minutes.

1. You will need ¼ yard of felt for the bear shape, scraps of felt for the foot pads and bow, embroidery thread for facial features, and sewing thread.

2. Cut three felt shapes in brown or whatever color you want your teddy bear to be. You will have back, front, and face. If using pinking shears, cut just outside pattern lines (Figs. 7-22A and 7-22B).

3. Cut foot pads of appropriate color. Mine are a warm beige.

4. Cut bow in a bright-colored felt.

5. Cut a shape of any color felt as filler using the back pattern but slightly smaller.

6. Pin all pieces together, right sides out, filler in the center of the sandwich. The bow nestles just under the chin. Stitch by machine or whipstitch by hand around the outer edge, leaving the chin unstitched so that you can embroider the face by hand. The nose may be a bit of felt or be embroidered.

7. When you have finished the face, secure the bow and chin with stitching and add foot pads.

8. By hand, sew a loop at the top. Try the method discussed near the end of the free chevron project earlier in this chapter—zigzagging over a strip of fabric—using a color that matches your bear.

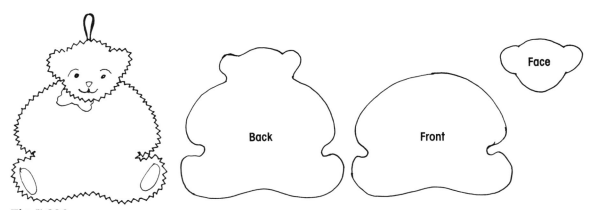

Fig. 7-22A.
Teddy bear potholder contour drawing guides.

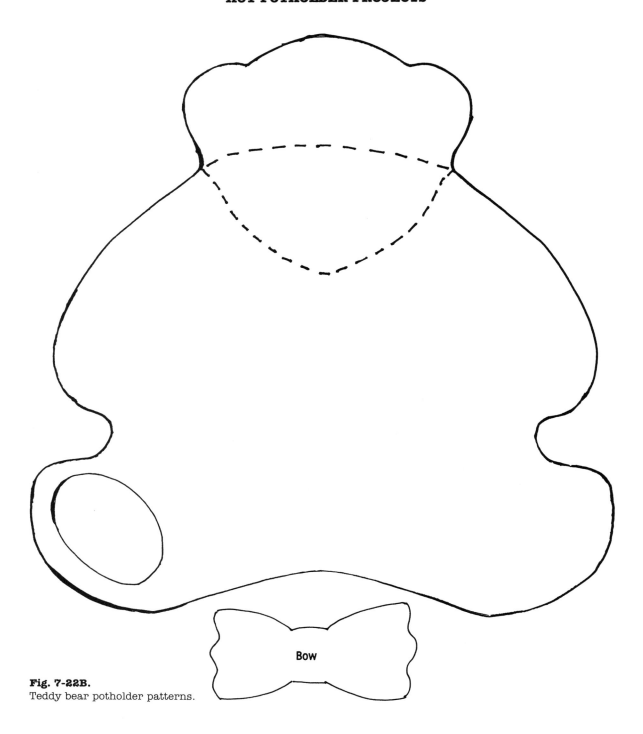

Bow

Fig. 7-22B.
Teddy bear potholder patterns.

Dragon Mitt

If you want a mitt to do double-duty as a hot-pot holder and as a puppet, try this dragon (Fig. 7-23), but only if you have time and patience. Make any color dragon your imagination dictates. Mine is green because that's the only prequilted fabric I had. His scales are several different green prints and solids. Since his mouth would be grasping smoking hot vessels, I chose a pink and orange fabric that looked as if he were already breathing fire. This fabric was not prequilted, so I layered it with cotton batting and another fabric and machine quilted it before cutting the mouth shape.

1. You will need ¼ yard each of two different colors of prequilted fabric, scraps of fabric for scales and eyes, a bit of paper-backed fusible web, bias tape for binding, and sewing thread.

2. Using Fig. 4-24 in chapter 4, cut two of piece A and one of piece B from prequilted fabric. Do not sew these at this time.

3. For scales, cut twenty pieces measuring 1½" by 2¾". These may be several different fabrics or all the same (Fig. 7-24a).

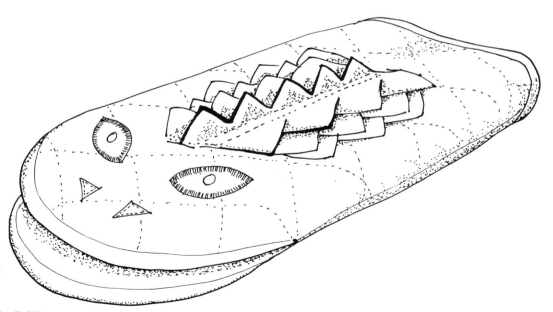

Fig. 7-23.
This dragon mitt can also be a hand puppet.

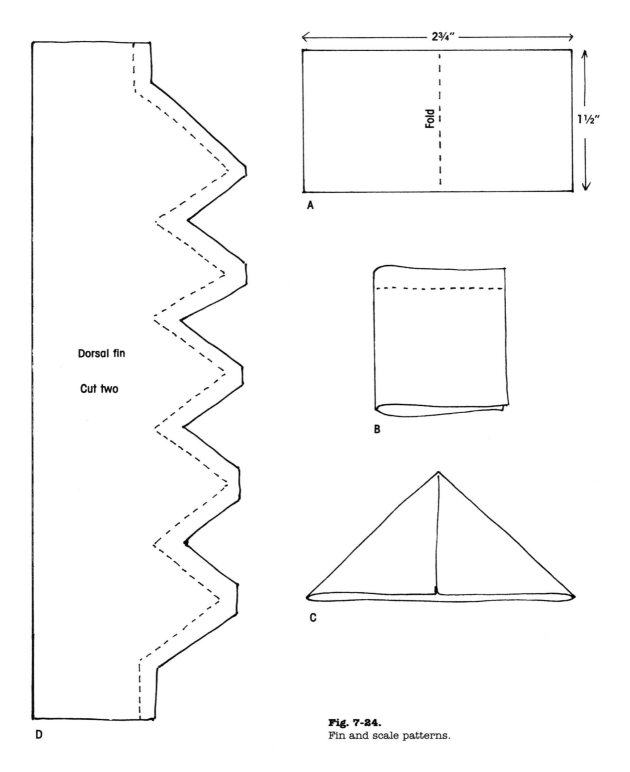

2¾″

Fold

1½″

A

B

C

Dorsal fin

Cut two

D

Fig. 7-24.
Fin and scale patterns.

4. Fold each scale in half crosswise, right sides together, and sew one side, making a ¼″ seam (Fig. 7-24b). Turn right side out and arrange so that seam is on back side of triangle (Fig. 7-24c). Do not press; the scales will stand up better if left unpressed.

5. For dorsal fin, cut two pieces by the pattern (Fig. 7-24d). With right sides together, sew along dotted line. Clip seams. Turn, poking peaks into sharp points. Open out flat, turn under short ends separately, and hem.

6. Mark center of one of piece A (Fig. 7-25a). Scales will be sewn on either side of this line, beginning with outside row, working toward center, and making three rows.

7. Sew three scales in a row ¾″ from centerline. Overlap scales about ½″.

8. New row will be ⅝″ from centerline, arranged with points in spaces between previous row's points.

9. Final row should be ½″ from centerline.

10. Sew scales on other side of centerline in same arrangement.

11. Lay dorsal fin down along centerline, with long edges folded under (Fig 7-25b) and covering raw edges of nearest row of scales. Sew along folded edge and again near the dorsal fin (Fig. 7-25c). Do the same on other side.

12. From fabric bonded with paper-backed fusible web, cut eyes and nostrils, iron them in place, and satin stitch around their edges. I used a polka dot fabric for eyes, giving my dragon a pink pupil in his yellow eye. Nostrils were fire-breathing orange.

13. Placing right sides together, sew 6½″ along side seams of A pieces (Fig. 7-26a). Fold one side back. Lay oval

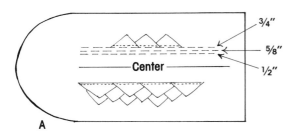

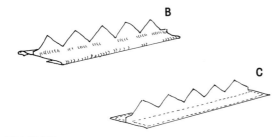

Fig. 7-25.
Sewing fin and scales.

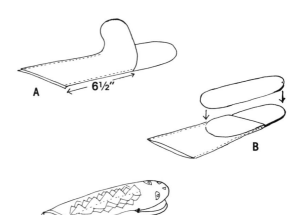

Fig. 7-26.
Assembly of dragon mitt.

shaped piece on oval formed by arch shapes, right sides together, to see if it fits (Fig. 7-26b). If it seems too small, you will need to take a few more stitches on side seam. Try for fit again. When you are satisfied with the fit, pin in place and stitch one arch at a time.

14. Turn right side out and hand stitch at corner of mouth to prevent mouth from gaping (Fig. 7-26c).

15. Bind the raw edge of mitt opening.

Your Label Is Showing

How many times have you seen someone neatly dressed but with one small exception—a clothing label turned out at the neckline proclaiming to all that the garment came from J. C. Penney, is a size 12, and should be tumble-dried? How often have you been mercilessly niggled by a label that is too stiff or scratchy? We often cut labels out of our garments and toss them into the trash. Why not save the next ones you clip and put them to decorative use?

Though I've seen labels suggested as embellishment for many years (Jean Ray Laury being the first in *Quilts and Coverlets*, Van Nostrand Rheinhold, 1970), I haven't seen them on potholders. So here goes.

You will have to decide on the size of your potholder, dictated, perhaps, by the number and size of your labels. I used nineteen labels on a 7½″ square (Fig. 7-27). In cutting labels from clothing you plan to continue wearing, take care. It's easy to snip the garment or to destroy stitching that is crucial to the construction of the piece.

1. You will need fabric for back and front of potholder (how much depends on how big you want the potholder), labels, cotton batting, 1″-wide bias tape for binding, and sewing thread.

2. Choose a fabric of a color that complements the labels. My labels were mostly black or white. Touches of red suggested a red background. I didn't have a piece of red large enough, so I pieced three reds together for the background.

3. Arrange labels on background and pin them in place. You may want them in a tight arrangement with no background showing through, but since my labels were rather somber, I left space in between for lots of red to shine. Though I aligned all my labels as if the letters were typed on a page, experiment turning them at right angles or on a slant.

4. Stitch labels to background fabric. Some are well constructed, with selvages and the ends turned under. A straight stitch will suffice for these. Others have raw or frayed edges and will require a narrow zigzag.

5. Cut batting and a backing fabric the same size as the labeled front.

6. Pin these layers together with right sides out and filler in between.

7. Machine quilt between labels.

8. Bind according to instructions in chapter 4's section on tape binding with mitered corners.

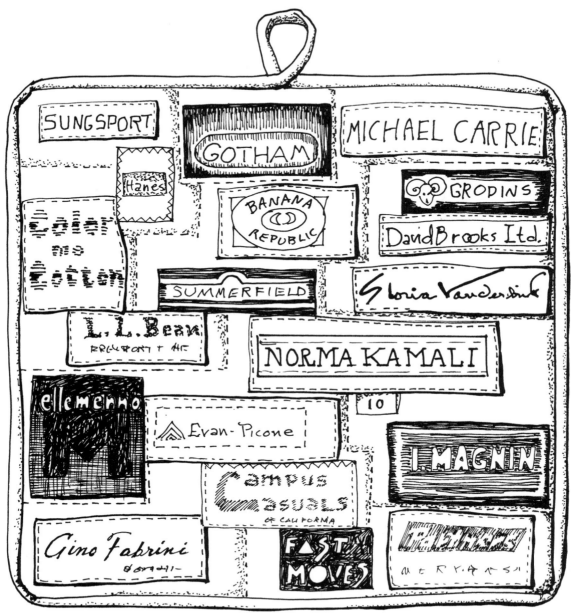

Fig. 7-27.
Label potholder.

Blue Plate Special

You may be too young to remember a listing on the menus of inexpensive restaurants called the Blue Plate Special. I don't know why it was called that, because it wasn't necessarily served on a blue plate, but the name indicated a plate lunch of meat, mashed potatoes, and a green vegetable, with perhaps a slice of tomato in season—all for a modest price. It might include a cup of coffee or iced tea and a piece of pie. Anyway, that's the inspiration for this potholder (Fig. 7-28). Construction is by Janie Warnick's method.

Fig. 7-28.
Blue Plate Special.

1. You will need ¼ yard of blue fabric, filler of your choice, scraps of fabric in colors to suggest your food menu, a small piece of paper-backed fusible web, 5″ of fabric for closure, and sewing thread.

2. Cut two circles of blue fabric 6½″ in diameter. A solid fabric rather than a print will present the food to better advantage.

3. Trace a 5″ circle centered on the front circle.

4. Cut filler about 6″ in diameter.

5. When you have chosen fabrics to represent the foods, bond them to paper-backed fusible web. Cut the shapes by my pattern (Fig. 7-29) or devise your own. Then bond them to the front circle, within the 5″ marked circle, and appliqué with a straight stitch or zigzag.

6. Pin filler to back side of front circle. If using quilt batting, back it with a piece of fabric so the batting will not catch on the feed dogs of your machine.

7. Stitch several rows of straight stitch over the marked circle. I stitched half the circle in dark blue thread and half in light blue to indicate the light and shadow of the plate's indentation.

8. Slash back circle of potholder about 3½″ on the straight grain.

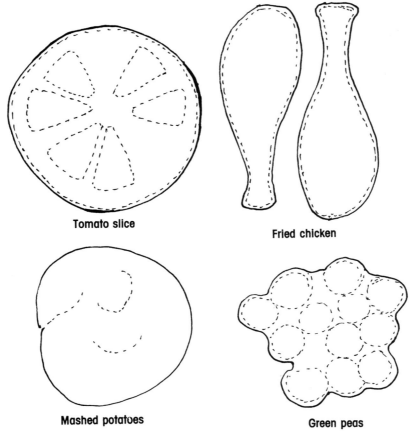

Tomato slice

Fried chicken

Mashed potatoes

Green peas

Fig. 7-29.
Patterns for Blue Plate Special foods.

9. Right sides together and with a loop pinned to the inside, sew around the perimeter with a ¼″ seam (or smaller, if you're comfortable with that).

10. Turn. Run a pointed instrument all around seam.

11. Bond a lighter blue fabric or a print to paper-backed fusible web and cut a 5″ circle from it. Bond this over the slash.

Some who remember the Blue Plate Special think it originated with plates in Blue Willow pattern, which was reproduced in restaurant ware. I happened to have some fabric printed in the Blue Willow pattern, so I made the back circle of that.

12. Stitch once more around the circle on the front, further defining the plate indentation.

Poetic Pocket Potholder

This piece is like the diagonal pocket mitt in chapter 4 but with a few adjustments to accommodate the quotation. White or light-colored fabrics are specified so that the printed quotation on the pocket may be read easily and so that the fabric that is underneath the pocket will not show through. The small contour drawings indicate the shapes to be cut from the full-size patterns.

1. You will need a 7″ square of denim, ¼ yard of white fabric such as canvas or duck, filler of your choice, a small piece of patterned fabric, and sewing thread.

2. Cut one piece blue denim and one piece white cotton fabric by contour drawing A, full size of potholder (Fig. 7-30). **Note:** You will need to enlarge the pattern in Fig. 7-30 on a copy machine at 110% to get a potholder 6¾″ square.

3. Cut filler ¼″ smaller all around than piece A.

4. Machine quilt filler to wrong side of denim.

5. Cut full-size piece the shape of drawing C in a patterned fabric.

6. Stitch C to one corner of white A piece by zigzagging the diagonal edge with an open spacing and straight stitching the outer edge close to the edge.

7. Cut B of firm white or pastel fabric. I used white canvas.

8. Bind diagonal edge of B with bias or straight-grain binding in contrasting color.

9. Use a Sharpie permanent marker with an extra fine point in black or a color to letter the quotation:

We may live without friends;
We may live without books;
But civilized man cannot
Live without cooks.
　　　　　　—Bulwer-Lytton

You might prefer this quotation:

Eat, drink, and be merry,
For tomorrow ye diet.
　　　　—William Gilmore Beymer

10. Pin B right side up to white piece A with patterned fabric showing at corner.

11. Pin above arrangement right side up over filler with denim right side down.

12. Straight stitch around outer edge. Then zigzag edge with satin stitch over a cord or use a narrow balanced serger stitch.

13. Make loop by satin stitching over a narrow strip of fabric, as in the free chevron project earlier in this chapter, and attach.

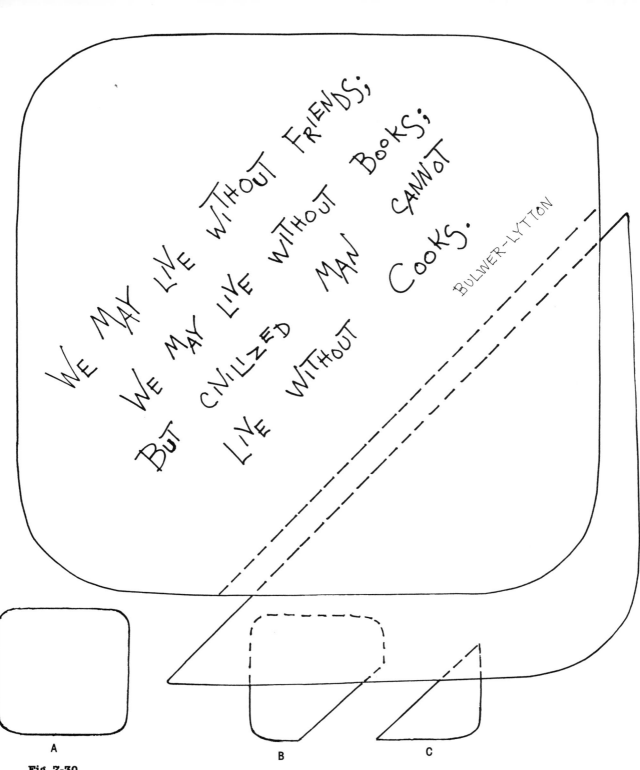

Fig. 7-30.
Pattern for poetic pocket mitt.

The Final Word

Now, *please* free yourself, if you haven't already, and stitch up a potholder like no one has ever seen. For once in your life, there are no rules to adhere to. If it functions as a potholder, it's a success. If it looks good, that's a bonus. If you had fun creating it, what more could you ask for? Just do it.

Appendix

Museums

If you wish to see potholders in the following museums, call or write first because what you want to see may not be on display. Most museums are understaffed and some smaller ones are run by volunteers, so be patient and understanding in making viewing arrangements. It may take months to arrange to see particular items. Many museums that I wrote to never answered, even though I sent a self-addressed, stamped envelope. I assume they did not have personnel to reply. The museums listed below have potholders in their collections:

Center for the History of American Needlework, P.O. Box 359, Valencia, Pennsylvania 16059.

Henry Francis DuPont Winterthur Museum, Winterthur, Delaware 19735.

National Museum of American History, Smithsonian Institution, Washington, D.C. 20560.

Oakland Museum, 1000 Oak Street, Oakland, California 94607.

Shelburne Museum, P.O. Box 10, Shelburne, Vermont 05482.

Sources for Supplies

Looper looms and cotton loopers are available from:

Dharma Trading Company, 1604 Fourth Street, San Rafael, California 94901 (415-456-1211). This address handles looms and loopers. For textile paints, pens, and markers see address on page 114.

Hearth Song, P.O. Box B, Sebastopol, California 95473.

Rug Weaving Supplies, P.O. Box 361, Augusta, Michigan 49012. Gray, white, and cream loopers only. No looms.

When ordering loopers from any source, be sure to specify cotton loopers.

Pretreated fabric for blueprinting is available from:

Blueprints-Printables, 1504 #7 Industrial Way, Belmont, California 94002 (800-356-0445).

Quilting items:

Keepsake Quilting, Rte. 25, P.O. Box 1618, Centre Harbor, New Hampshire 03226-1618. A complete source for quilting supplies, with outstanding service.

Quilting Bee, Department Ch, 375 Castro, Mountain View, California 94041. This store has everything—books, a vast array of fabrics, batts (both cotton and polyester), trims, and sewing machines. It does not have a catalogue, but if you send a scrap of fabric or describe what you want, store employees will try to accommodate.

Treadleart, 25834-1 Narbonne Avenue, Lomita, California 90717. Books, marking pens, fabric crayons, threads, and loads more. Ask for their catalogue, $3.

Versatex textile paints are available from:

Flax Art and Design, 1699 Market Street, P.O. Box 7216, San Francisco, California 94120-7216.

Dharma Trading Company, P.O. Box 15096, San Rafael, California 94915 (800-542-5227). These folks have all sorts of goodies for fiber artists. Ask for their free catalogue.

Createx textile paints are available from:

Color Craft, 14 Airport Park Road, East Granby, Connecticut 06026.

Dharma Trading Company (see address under Versatex).

Fiber art supplies—dyes, paints, brushes, and so on:

Cerulean Blue, P.O. Box 21168, Seattle, Washington 98111-3168. This is a rather sophisticated catalogue, geared toward those who know what they are doing, but it also offers products and information valuable to the novice.

Rubber stamps and inks appropriate for stamping on fabric:

Co-motion Rubber Stamps, 4455 S. Park Avenue, Suite 105, Tuscon, Arizona 85714-1669.

Fabric pens and markers:

Dharma Trading Company (see address under Versatex). Pigma Micron for an extra fine line, Fabricolor for a wide range of colors, Deka markers, and others.

Treadleart (see address under Quilting Items).

Instructions for crochet potholders:

Annie's Attic, Rt. 2, Box 212B, Big Sandy, Texas 75755.

References and Further Reading

Bradkin, Cheryl Greider. *Basic Seminole Patchwork*. Mountain View, Calif.: Leone Publications, 1991.

Coates-Clark, J. & P. O.N.T. Potholders Book No. 294.

Cooking Out-of-Doors. New York: Girl Scouts National Organization, 1946.

Dudley, Taimi. *Strip Patchwork*. New York: Van Nostrand Reinhold, 1980.

Fanning, Robbie, and Tony Fanning. *The Complete Book of Machine Embroidery*. Radnor, Pa.: Chilton, 1986.

———. *The Complete Book of Machine Quilting*. Radnor, Pa.: Chilton, 1980.

Gleason, Kay. *Stamp It!* New York: Van Nostrand Reinhold, 1981.

Gordon, Beverly. *Shaker Textile Arts*. Hanover, N.H.: University Press of New England, 1980.

APPENDIX

Gray, Isle. *Designing and Making Dolls.* New York: Watson-Guptil, 1972. *Handwoven Magazine*, Sept./Oct. 1991, p. 114.

———. May/June 1992, p. 104.

———. Jan./Feb. 1993, p. 104.

Hardie, Dee. "From Thornhill Farm." *House Beautiful* (May 1991).

Hein, Gisela. *Printing Fabric by Hand.* New York: Van Nostrand Reinhold, 1972.

Herr, Patricia T. "Twwerich Un Ender." In *Bits and Pieces: Textile Traditions.* Edited by Jeanette Lasansky. Lewisburg, Pa.: Oral Traditions Project of the Union County Historical Society, 1991.

Hoover, Doris. "Easy Fabric Painting for Quiltmakers." *Quilter's Newsletter* (May 1983).

Laury, Jean Ray. *Dollmaking: A Creative Approach.* New York: Van Nostrand Reinhold, 1970.

———. *Imagery on Fabric.* Martinez, Calif.: C and T Publishing, 1992.

———. *Quilts and Coverlets: A Contemporary Approach.* New York: Van Nostrand Reinhold, 1970.

Maines, Rachel. "Textiles as History." In *American Quilts: A Handmade Legacy.* Edited by L. Thomas Frye. Oakland, Calif.: Oakland Museum Historical Department, 1981.

Marsh, Jan. *Jane and May Morris: A Biographical Story 1839–1938.* London: Pandora Press, 1986.

Montgomery Ward Catalogue No. 57. Reprint. Mineola, N.Y.: Dover, 1895.

RSM Enterprises. *Rubberstampmadness.* (September/October 1989; January/February 1992; March/April 1992).

Sears Roebuck 1902 Catalogue. Reprint. New York: Bounty Books.

Swan, Susan. *Plain and Fancy: American Women and Their Needlework 1700 to 1850.* New York: Holt, 1977.

Warnick, Jane and Jackie Dodson. *Gifts Galore.* Radnor, Pa.: Chilton, 1992.

Index

INDEX